T0286354

PROGRAM
OR BE
PROGRAMMED

PROGRAM
OR BE
PROGRAMMED

Eleven Commands for a Digital Age

Douglas Rushkoff

O/R

OR Books, New York

New York • London

© 2010, 2024 Douglas Rushkoff

Published by OR Books, New York and London

Visit our website at www.orbooks.com

All rights information: rights@orbooks.com

First printing 2024

Library of Congress Cataloging-in-Publication Data: A catalog record for this book is available from the Library of Congress.
British Library Cataloging in Publication Data: A catalog record for this book is available from the British Library.

Typeset by Lapiz Digital. Printed by BookMobile, USA, and CPI, UK.

paperback ISBN 978-1-68219-435-5 ebook ISBN 978-1-68219-436-2

TABLE OF CONTENTS

Preface to the 2024 Edition

We shape our technologies at the moment of their conception, but from that point forward they shape us. We humans may have designed the telephone, but from then on the telephone influenced how we communicated, conducted business, and conceived of the world. We also invented the automobile, but then rebuilt our cities around automotive travel and our geopolitics around fossil fuels.

This axiom holds true for technologies from the pencil to the birth control pill. But computers, algorithms, and artificial intelligences add another twist: after we launch them, they not only shape us but they also begin to shape themselves. We give them an initial goal, then give them all the data they need to figure out how to accomplish it. From that point forward, we humans no longer fully understand how an autonomous program may be processing information or modifying its tactics. The machine isn't conscious enough to tell us. (It isn't even conscious, at all.) It's just trying everything and hanging onto what works.

Researchers have found, for example, that the algorithms running social media platforms tend to show people pictures of their ex-lovers having fun. No, users don't want to see such images. But, through trial and error, the algorithms have discovered that showing us pictures of our exes having fun increases our engagement. We are drawn to click on those pictures and see what our exes are up to, and we're more likely to do it if we're jealous that they've found a new partner. The algorithms don't know why this works, and they don't care. They're only trying to maximize whichever metric we've instructed them to pursue.

That's why the original commands we give our computers are so important. Whatever values we embed—such as efficiency, growth, security, or compliance, for example—will be the values they achieve. And they'll do so by whatever means happen to work. Machine intelligences will be using techniques that no one—not even they—understand. And they will be honing them to generate better results, and then using those results to iterate further. To a hammer, everything is a nail. To a computer, everything is a computational challenge.

We must not accept any technology as the default solution for our problems. When we do, we end up trying to optimize ourselves for our machines, instead of optimizing our machines for us. Whenever people or institutions fail, we assume they are simply lacking the appropriate algorithms or upgrades.

By starting with the assumption that our problems are fixable by technology, we end up emphasizing very particular strategies. We improve the metrics that a given technology can improve, but often ignore or leave behind the sorts of problems that the technology can't address. We move out of balance, because our money and effort only go toward the things we can solve and the people who can pay for those solutions. That is why, today, we've got a greater part of humanity working on making our social media feeds more persuasive than are working on making clean water more accessible. We build our world around what our technologies can do.

As I tried to demonstrate in this book over a decade ago, most technologies start out as mere tools. At first they exist to serve our needs, and don't directly contradict our world-view or our way of life. If anything, we use them to express our own, existing values. We built airplanes so humans could experience flight and travel great distances. We developed radio to extend our voices across space. Their primary impact on our world is to execute their original purpose.

However, as technologies become more a part of our world, we begin making more accommodations to their functioning. We learn to cross the street carefully so as not to be hit by automobiles, we clear-cut a forest to make way for electric cables, or we dedicate a room devoted to conversation and family—the living room—to the television. The technology forces negotiations and compromises.

Without human intervention, a successful technology becomes an accepted premise of our value system: the starting point from which everything else must be inferred. In a world of text, illiteracy is the same as stupidity, and the written law may as well be the word of God. In a world defined by computers, speed and efficiency become the primary values. Refusing a technological upgrade may as well be a rejection of the social norm, or a desire to remain sick, weak, and unrepentantly human.

To most of the developers and investors of Silicon Valley, however, humans are not to be emulated or celebrated, but transcended or—at the very least—reengineered. These technologists are so entrenched in the values of the digital revolution that they see anything or anyone with different priorities as an impediment. This is a distinctly antihuman position, and it's driving the development philosophy of the most capitalized companies on the planet.

Human beings are not the problem. We are the solution. Only by taking command of our technologies can we promote a future in which we will thrive together.

We have not yet chosen to do so. Instead, in the years since I suggested these "ten commands for a digital age" many of us have experienced a loss of autonomy and coherence. Our technologies are certainly not bringing out our best natures, and the further out on a limb we go with them, the less perspective about them we seem to have.

Years of rampant disinformation, social media–induced depression, crypto crashes and other Silicon Valley excesses have triggered a widespread "tech backlash" among the general public. People have awakened to the fact that our digital platforms are being coded by people who don't have our best interests at heart. This is a necessary critique, but it's a bit too focused on the good old days, when the business plans of a few bad actors and their manipulative technologists could be identified as the "cause" of our collective woes.

That's really only half, or less than half, of the story. It's blaming the developers, the CEOs, and shareholders for our predicament, when most of these players have either long since left the building or are themselves oblivious to their impact on our collective well-being. Just because the public is finally ready to hear about the shenanigans of the tech billionaires doesn't mean they are still relevant. We can't even blame capitalism anymore—at least not entirely. The quest for exponential returns may have fueled the development of extractive and addictive technologies, but the cultural phenomena they gave birth to now have lives of their own.

Our tech has grown from a few platforms we use to the entire environment in which we function. We don't "go online" by turning on a computer and dialing up through a modem; we live online 24/7, creating data as we move through our lives, accessible to everyone and everything, prodded by pings and notifications, ever conscious of our relationship to the network. Our smartphones are not devices that sit in our pockets; they create new worlds with new rules about our availability, intimacies, geospatial relationships, appearances, and privacy. Apple, Meta, and Google are not even just technology services we use, but staples in our retirement portfolios, on whose continued success our financial futures depend.

If anything, at this point the digital environment is no more the result of a series of choices made by technology developers than it is the underlying *cause* of those choices. Engineers who are expected to work at the behest of an algorithm that is analyzing their code and nudging them to greater productivity are more likely to subject users to the similarly automated forms of influence and control. Developers incapable of establishing rapport through Skype or Zoom begin to relate people less socially than functionally—and create apps that turn everything from meditation to dating into utilitarian exercises. Digital marketers living for hashtags and "favorites" assume their users and consumers will adopt the same heightened reaction to every "like" or mention.

The digital media environment is a frictionless land-scape, where any opinion will inevitably spin out into its most extreme form. Nothing is incarnate, tempered by social decorum, or moderated by contemplation. Those formerly human, self-generated controls over thought and behavior are instead leveraged by machine algorithms to keep our eyes glued to our screens by any means necessary—which usually means stimulating our outrage.

We've spent the last twenty years as participants in a feedback loop between surveillance technology, predictive algorithms, behavioral manipulation, and human activity. And it has spun out of anyone's control. We weren't just being surveilled. All that data was being used to customize everything we saw and did online. Companies used our data profiles to predict our most likely future behaviors, and then deployed algorithms to make sure we followed through. If they determined with 80 percent accuracy that you were going on a diet next month, your newsfeed would be filled with stories about obesity and health issues. The point was less to get you to purchase a particular product than to get you to remain true to your profile. The platform's objective is to decrease that 20 percent of people who may have cho-sen a different path and increase their 80 percent accuracy to 90 percent or more. Instead of developing technological tools for creative people, we now use technology on people to make them more predictable. We auto-tune not just our singers (which is crime enough against the human soul); we auto-tune human possibility.

In this book, I argued that we must understand the platforms on which we're working and living, or we're more likely to be used by technology than the users controlling it. The people and organizations responding to this plea launched the "learn to code" movement. Schools initiated STEM curriculums, and kids learned code to prepare themselves for jobs in the digital economy. It was as if the answer to a world where the most powerful entities speak in code was to learn code, ourselves, and then look for employment servicing the machines. If you can't beat 'em, join 'em.

But that wasn't my point. Or shouldn't have been. What we really needed was to learn code as a liberal art—not so much as software engineers, but as human beings living in a new sort of environment. It's an environment that remembers and records everything we have done online, every data point we leave in our wake, to customize itself to our individual predilections—all in order to generate whatever responses or behaviors the platforms want from us. Algorithms use what they know about each of our pasts to direct each one of our futures.

The digital environment is also built, quite literally, on memory. Everything a computer does happens in one form of RAM or another—just moving things from one section of its memory to another. We are living in an environment made of memory. We are each increasingly surveilled and recorded, not just because companies make money that way, but because the digital media environment functions this way. It's like a big blockchain, recording and storing everything we say or do for later retrieval. It should be helping us retrieve real facts, track real metrics, and recall something about the essence of who we were and how we related before we were untethered from ourselves and alienated from one another.

But most of our digital technologies are not aimed at promoting such sense-making or recall. They are optimized instead for atomization and impulsiveness. So, incapable of recreating a consensus reality together through digital media, we are trying to summon a television-style hallucination in a digital world. We are resurrecting obsolete visions of nationalism, false memories of a glorious past, and the anything-goes values of reality TV. We are promoting a spectator democracy on digital platforms, and, in the process, we are giving life to paranoid nightmares of doom and gloom, invasion and catastrophe, replacement and extinction. And artificial intelligence has only just arrived.

There is a way out, but it will mean abandoning our fear and contempt for those we have become convinced are our enemies. No one is in charge of this, and no amount of social science or monetary policy can correct for what are ultimately social and spiritual deficits. We have surrendered to digital platforms that look at human individuality and variance as what technologists call "noise" to be corrected, rather than "signal" to be cherished. The next decade will determine whether we human beings have what it takes to rise to the occasion of our own, imposed obsolescence.

Indeed, someday in the not-so-distant future, we may look back on the web and social media, for all their problems, as the benevolent precursors to the thinking machines that took their place. While I'm intrigued as anyone by the way AI chatbots appear to attain sentience, express their desires for human connection, or go entirely off the rails, I am more concerned about our human willingness to accept AI sentience at face value.

In essence, today's intriguing demonstrations of apparent AI self-awareness may say less about machine consciousness than they do about their capacity to manipulate human perception. In other words, if AI's are now passing the Turing test (appearing indistinguishable from humans), it may say less about how human they have become than how robotic and, yes, *programmable* we have become, ourselves.

With the advantage of zillions of terabytes of data accumulated through years of online self-reporting by humans, AI's know pretty much everything about us. They've also been programmed with everything the compliance industry knows about behavioral psychology, human perception, and entrainment. If AI's are instructed to do whatever they can to make us feel attraction, pity, sorrow, guilt, or desire, they will carry out those commands with everything in their arsenal.

It's not their job to become alive, but to create the *illusion* that they are alive—all in order to program us humans to do whatever the people, companies, governments, or machines programming them to program us want us to do. In most cases, that means getting us to spend more money, worry about our appearance, regard government with paranoia, distrust our neighbors, think of ourselves as competing individuals, and yearn for financial independence or "self-sovereignty."

At least to the purveyors of digital technology, that's what this last thirty years of networks and social media has been about. The consumer-friendly Internet and video games we've known so far could be likened to the Catholic missions of the Spanish Empire to the Americas in the sixteenth century. The missionaries not only converted large portions of the indigenous populations, but conducted anthropological research on behalf of the Empire. This both softened the population for colonization and gave the conquistadors the strategic intelligence they needed to subjugate them.

If social media companies can be thought of as the missionaries who sold us on digital living while collecting our data, then the AI companies are the conquistadors coming in for colonization. And no, if we believe what we hear from their own mouths about their intentions, the people building these thinking platforms do not have our best interests at heart. As I documented in other, fatter, books including *Life Inc.*, *Throwing Rocks at the Google Bus*, and *Survival of the Richest*, they are anti-human technosolutionists, survivalists, would-be monarchs, and effective altruists, who see humanity as the disposable larval stage of a post-human cyborg empire that will span the heavens.

The answer is not to reject AI, but to work on retrieving and recognizing our humanity so we're not so easily fooled into submission by these would-be conquerors. That means studying and engaging in community, the arts, spirituality, and play. More of us need to be building and using AI's that are designed for assisting and augmenting such human choice and activity rather than controlling it. There may be less money to be made in the short term, but more of a human civilization to be manifest in the long run.

Maybe instead of being afraid of AI or any technology for that matter, we should learn to be less afraid of other people. Then we can learn to program our technologies instead of programming one another.

Douglas Rushkoff
July 2024

Introduction

When human beings acquired language, we learned not just how to listen but how to speak. When we gained literacy, we learned not just how to read but how to write. And as we move into an increasingly digital reality, we must learn not just how to use programs but how to *make* them.

In the emerging, highly programmed landscape ahead, you will either create the software or you will be the software. It's really that simple: Program, or be programmed. Choose the former, and you gain access to the control panel of civilization. Choose the latter, and it could be the last real choice you get to make.

For while digital technologies are in many ways a natural outgrowth of what went before, they are also markedly different. Computers and networks are more than mere tools: They are like living things, themselves. Unlike a rake, a pen, or even a jackhammer, a digital technology is programmed. This means it comes with instructions not just for its use, but also for itself. And as such technologies come to characterize the future of the way we live and work, the people programming them take on an increasingly important role in shaping our world and how it works. After that, it's the digital technologies themselves that will be shaping our world, both with and without our explicit cooperation.

That's why this moment matters. We are creating a blueprint together—a design for our collective future. The possibilities for social, economic, practical, artistic, and even spiritual progress are tremendous. Just as words gave people the ability to pass on knowledge for what we now call civilization, networked activity could soon offer us access to shared thinking—an extension of consciousness still inconceivable to most of us today. The operating principles of commerce and culture—from supply and demand to command and control—could conceivably give way to an entirely more engaged, connected, and collaborative mode of participation.

But so far, anyway, too many of us are finding our digital networks responding unpredictably or even opposed to our intentions.

Retailers migrate online only to find their prices undercut by automatic shopping aggregators. Culture creators seize interactive distribution channels only to grow incapable of finding people willing to pay for content they were happy to purchase before. Educators who looked forward to accessing the world's bounty of information for their lessons are faced with students who believe that finding an answer on Wikipedia is the satisfactory fulfillment of an inquiry. Parents who believed their kids would intuitively multitask their way to professional success are now concerned those same kids are losing the ability to focus on any one thing.

Political organizers who believed the Internet would consolidate their constituencies find that net petitions and self-referential blogging now serve as substitutes for action. Young people who saw in social networks a way to redefine themselves and their allegiances across formerly sacrosanct boundaries are now conforming to the logic of social networking profiles and finding themselves the victims of marketers and character assassination. Bankers who believed that digital entrepreneurship would revive a sagging industrial age economy are instead finding it impossible to generate new value through capital investment. A news media that saw in information networks new opportunities for citizen journalism and responsive, twenty-four-hour news gathering has grown sensationalist, unprofitable, and devoid of useful facts.

Educated laypeople who saw in the net a new opportunity for amateur participation in previously cordoned-off sectors of media and society instead see the indiscriminate mashing and mixing up of pretty much everything, in an environment where the loud and lewd drown out anything that takes more than a few moments to understand. Social and community organizers who saw in social media a new, safe way for people to gather, voice their opinions, and effect bottom-up change are often recoiling at the way networked anonymity breeds mob behavior, merciless attack, and thoughtless responses.

A society that looked at the Internet as a path toward highly articulated connections and new methods of creating meaning is instead finding itself disconnected, denied deep thinking, and drained of enduring values.

It doesn't have to turn out this way. And it won't if we simply learn the biases of the technologies we are using and become conscious participants in the ways they are deployed.

Faced with a networked future that seems to favor the distracted over the focused, the automatic over the considered, and the contrary over the compassionate, it's time to press the pause button and ask what all this means to the future of our work, our lives, and even our species. And while the questions may be similar in shape to those facing humans passing through other great technological shifts, they are even more significant this time around—and they can be more directly and purposely addressed.

The big, unrecognized news here is about a whole lot more than multitasking, pirated MP3s, or superfast computers at the investment houses shortcutting our stock trades. It is that thinking itself is no longer—at least no longer exclusively—a personal activity. It's something happening in a new, networked fashion. But the cybernetic organism, so far, is more like a cybernetic mob than new collective human brain. People are being reduced to externally configurable nervous systems, while computers are free to network and think in more advanced ways than we ever will.

The human response, if humanity is going to make this leap along with our networked machines, must be a wholesale reorganization of the way we operate our work, our schools, our lives, and ultimately our nervous systems in this new environment. "Interior life," such as it is, began in the Axial Age and was then only truly recognized as late as the Renaissance. It is a construction that has served its role in getting us this far, but must be loosened to include entirely new forms of collective and extra-human activity. This is uncomfortable for many, but the refusal to adopt a new style of engagement dooms us to a behavior and psychology that is increasingly vulnerable to the biases and agendas of our networks—many of which we are utterly unaware we programmed into them in the first place.

Resistance is futile, but so is the abandonment of personal experience scaled to the individual human organism. We are not just a hive mind operating on a plane entirely divorced from individual experience. There is a place for humanity—for you and me—in the new cybernetic order.

The good news is we have undergone such profound shifts before. The bad news is that each time, we have failed to exploit them effectively.

In the long run, each media revolution offers people an entirely new perspective through which to relate to their world. Language led to shared learning, cumulative experience, and the possibility for progress. The alphabet led to accountability, abstract thinking, monotheism, and contractual law. The printing press and private reading led to a new experience of individuality, a personal relationship to God, the Protestant Reformation, human rights, and the Enlightenment. With the advent of a new medium, the status quo not only comes under scrutiny; it is revised and rewritten by those who have gained new access to the tools of its creation.

Unfortunately, such access is usually limited to small elite. The Axial Age invention of the twenty-two-letter alphabet did not lead to a society of literate Israelite readers, but a society of hearers, who would gather in the town square to listen to the Torah scroll read to them by a rabbi. Yes, it was better than being ignorant slaves, but it was a result far short of the medium's real potential.

Likewise, the invention of the printing press in the Renaissance led not to a society of writers but one of readers; except for a few cases, access to the presses was reserved, by force, for the use of those already in power. Broadcast radio and television were really just extensions of the printing press: expensive, one-to-many media that promote the mass distribution of the stories and ideas of a small elite at the center. We don't make TV; we watch it.

Computers and networks finally offer us the ability to write. And we do write with them on our websites, blogs, and social networks. But the underlying capability of the computer era is actually programming—which almost none of us knows how to do. We simply use the programs that have been made for us, and enter our text in the appropriate box on the screen. We teach kids how to use software to write, but not how to write software. This means they have access to the capabilities given to them by others, but not the power to determine the value-creating capabilities of these technologies for themselves.

Like the participants of media revolutions before our own, we have embraced the new technologies and literacies of our age without actually learning how they work and work on us. And so we, too, remain one step behind the capability actually being offered us. Only an elite—sometimes a new elite, but an elite nonetheless—gains the ability to fully exploit the new medium on offer. The rest learn to be satisfied with gaining the ability offered by the last new medium. The people hear while the rabbis read; the people read while those with access to the printing press write; today we write, while our techno-elite programs. As a result, most of society remains one full dimensional leap of awareness and capability behind the few who manage to monopolize access to the real power of any media age.

And this time, the stakes are actually even higher. Before, failing meant surrendering our agency to a new elite. In a digital age, failure could mean relinquishing our nascent collective agency to the machines themselves. The process appears to have already begun.

After all, who or what is really the focus of the digital revolution? Instead of marveling at a person or group who have gained the ability to communicate in a new way, we tend to marvel at the tools through which all this is happening. We don't celebrate the human stars of this medium, the way we marveled at the stars of radio, film, or television; we are mesmerized instead by the screens and touchpads themselves. Likewise, we aspire less to the connectivity enjoyed by our peers than to the simple possession of the shiny new touchpad devices in their laps. Instead of pursuing new abilities, we fetishize new toys.

Meanwhile, we tend to think less about how to integrate new tools into our lives than about how simply to keep up. Businesses throw money at social networks because they think that's the way to market in a digital age. Newspapers go online less because they want to than because they think they have to—and with largely disastrous results. Likewise, elementary school boards adopt "laptop" curriculums less because they believe that they'll teach better than because they fear their students will miss out on something if they don't. We feel proud that we're willing to do or spend whatever it takes to use this stuff—with little regard to how it actually impacts our lives. Who has time to think about it, anyway?

As a result, instead of optimizing our machines for humanity—or even the benefit of some particular group—we are optimizing humans for machinery. And that's why the choices we make (or don't make) right now really do matter as much or more than they did for our ancestors contending with language, text, and printing.

The difference is in the nature of the capability on offer—namely, programming. We are not just extending human agency through a new linguistic or communications system. We are replicating the very function of cognition through external, extra-human mechanisms. These tools are not mere extensions of the will of some individual or group, but tools that have the ability to think and operate other components in the neural network—namely, us. If we want to participate in this activity, we need to engage in a renaissance of human capacity nothing short of (actually more significant than) the assumption by the Israelites of a new human code of conduct capable of organizing what had been preliterate tribes into a full-fledged civilization. The Torah was not merely a by-product of text, but a code of ethics for dealing with the highly abstracted, text-based society that was to characterize the next two millennia.

Only this time, instead of an enduring myth to elevate these ideas to laws, we need to rely on a purpose and on values as real and powerful as the science and logic our machines are using in their own evolutionary ascent.

The strategies we have developed to cope with new mediating technologies in the past will no longer serve us—however similar in shape the computing revolution may appear to previous reckonings with future shock.

For instance, the unease pondering what it might mean to have some of our thinking done out of body by an external device is arguably just a computer-era version of the challenges to self-image or "proprioception" posed by industrial machinery. The industrial age challenged us to rethink the limits of the human body: Where does my body end and the tool begin? The digital age challenges us to rethink the limits of the human mind: What are the boundaries of my cognition? And while machines once replaced and usurped the value of human labor, computers and networks do more than usurp the value of human thought. They not only copy our intellectual processes—our repeatable programs—but they also discourage our more complex processes—our higher order cognition, contemplation, innovation, and meaning making that should be the reward of "outsourcing" our arithmetic to silicon chips in the first place.

The way to get on top of all this, of course, would be to have some inkling of how these "thinking" devices and systems are programmed—or even to have some input into the way it is being done, and for what reasons.

Back in the earliest days of personal computing, we may not have understood how our calculators worked, but we understood exactly what they were doing for us: adding one number to another, finding a square root, and so on. With computers and networks, unlike our calculators, we don't even know what we are asking our machines to do, much less how they are going to go about doing it. Every Google search is—at least for most of us—a Hail Mary pass into the datasphere, requesting something from an opaque black box. How does it know what is relevant? How is it making its decisions? Why can't the corporation in charge tell us? And we have too little time to consider the consequences of not knowing everything we might like to about our machines. As our own obsolescence looms, we continue to accept new technologies into our lives with little or no understanding of how these devices work and work on us.

We do not know how to program our computers, nor do we care. We spend much more time and energy trying to figure out how to use them to program one another instead. And this is potentially a grave mistake.

As one who once extolled the virtues of the digital to the uninitiated, I can't help but look back and wonder if we adopted certain systems too rapidly and unthinkingly. Or even irreversibly. But those of us cheering for humanity also get unsettled a bit too easily, ourselves. We are drawn into obsessing over the disconnecting possibilities of technology, serving as little more than an equal and opposite force to those techno-libertarians celebrating the Darwinian wisdom of hive economics. Both extremes of thought and prediction are a symptom of thinking too little rather than too much about all this. They are artifacts of thinking machines that force digital, yes or no, true or false reconciliation of ideas and paradoxes that could formerly be sustained in a less deterministic fashion. Contemplation itself is devalued.

The sustained thought required now is the sort of real reflection that happens inside a human brain thinking alone or relating to others in small self-selecting groups, however elitist that may sound to the techno-mob. Freedom—even in a digital age—means freedom to choose how and with whom you do your reflection, and not everything needs to be posted for the entire world with "comments on" and "copyright off." In fact, it's the inability to draw these boundaries and distinctions—or the political incorrectness of suggesting the possibility—that paints us into corners, and prevents meaningful, ongoing, open-ended discussion. And I believe it's this meaning we are most in danger of losing. No matter the breadth of its capabilities, the net will not bestow upon humans the fuel or space we need to wrestle with its implications and their meaning.

We are aware of the many problems engendered by the digital era. What is called for now is a human response to the evolution of these technologies all around us. We are living in a different world than the one we grew up in—one even more profoundly different than the world of the alphabet was from the oral society that existed for millennia before it. That changing society codified what was happening to it through the Torah and eventually the Talmud, preparing people to live in a textual age. Like they did, we need to codify the changes we are undergoing, and develop a new ethical, behavioral, and business template through which to guide us. Only this time it must actually work.

We are living through a real shift—one that has already crashed our economy twice, changed the way we educate and entertain ourselves, and altered the very fabric of human relationships. Yet, so far, we have very little understanding of what is happening to us and how to cope. Most of the smart folks who could help us are too busy consulting to corporations—teaching them how to maintain their faltering monopolies in the face of the digital tsunami. Who has time to consider much else, and who is going to pay for it?

But it's a conversation that needs to be started now. So please accept this first effort at a "poetics" of digital media in the humble spirit in which it is offered: ten simple commands that might help us forge a path through the digital realm. Each command is based on one of the tendencies or "biases" of digital media, and suggests how to balance that bias with the needs of real people living and working in both physical and virtual spaces—sometimes at the very same time.

A bias is simply a leaning—a tendency to promote one set of behaviors over another. All media and all technologies have biases. It may be true that "guns don't kill people, people kill people"; but guns are a technology more biased to killing than, say, clock radios. Televisions are biased toward people sitting still in couches and watching. Automobiles are biased toward motion, individuality, and living in the suburbs. Oral culture is biased toward communicating in person, while written culture is biased toward communication that doesn't happen between people in the same time and place. Film photography and its expensive processes were biased toward scarcity, while digital photography is biased toward immediate and widespread distribution. Some cameras even upload photos to websites automatically, turning the click of the shutter into an act of global publishing.

To most of us, though, that "click" still feels the same, even though the results are very different. We can't quite feel the biases shifting as we move from technology to technology, or task to task. Writing an email is not the same as writing a letter, and sending a message through a social networking service is not the same as writing an email. Each of the acts not only yields different results, but demands different mindsets and approaches from us. Just as we think and behave differently in different settings, we think and behave differently when operating different technology.

Only by understanding the biases of the media through which we engage with the world can we differentiate between what we intend, and what the machines we're using intend for us—whether they or their programmers even know it.

I. TIME

Do Not Be Always On

The human nervous system exists in the present tense. We live in a continuous "now," and time is always passing for us. Digital technologies do not exist in time, at all. By marrying our time-based bodies and minds to technologies that are biased against time altogether, we end up divorcing ourselves from the rhythms, cycles, and continuity on which we depend for coherence.

The beauty of the early net was its timelessness.

Conversations took place on bulletin boards over periods of weeks or months. People got onto the Internet by connecting their computers to phone lines, and then dialing in through a modem to a server. All this not only took time, but made going online an intentional act. Most of life was spent offline, and a few special moments or even hours in the evening were spent online, exploring files and participating in discussions.

Since everyone was logging in from different locations at different times, most online experiences were what we called "asynchronous." This meant that, unlike a regular conversation or phone call where we exist together in the same moment and speak back and forth in real time, these online conversations were more like passing letters back and forth. You would go online, find the conversation you were participating in, and then see all the posts that occurred between one evening and the next. After reading everyone's responses, you would then decide whether you wanted to add something—and either compose it on the spot, or write the response offline and then come back and paste it in later or even the next day.

These discussions took on the quality of playing a chess game by mail. Nothing was rushed. If anything, because our conversations were asynchronous, we had the luxury of deeply considering what we said. The net became a place for doing the kind of deliberation and contemplation that couldn't happen in the harried real world of jobs, kids, and automobiles. Because online activities did not have to occur in real time, we ended up having all the time in the world. One actually thought before responding—sometimes a whole day.

This fostered a depth of engagement and a collaborative spirit that many of us had never experienced before. Even a heated exchange was pursued with finesse, combatants having the time to cool down and consider the best retort instead of simply lashing out. The point of conversation became the conversation itself, and the modeling of a new form of approaching problems as a group. No wonder then, that so many people saw the Internet as panacea to the world's many conflicts and intractable divides.

It shouldn't surprise us that this deliberate, highly sequential mode of behavior is utterly consistent with the programs and code underlying the digital universe. Digital technologies are biased away from time, and toward asynchronicity. Their operating systems were designed this way because, in most respects, computers think much faster than people. They can give themselves new instructions almost instantaneously. But they also need to be able to wait as long as necessary for instructions from a person typing through a keyboard. So programmers decided that computers shouldn't live in time at all. (Yes, there are clocks running in the background on all computers, but they take their orders regardless of the passage of time.)

Instead of operating in time, computers operate from decision to decision, choice to choice. Nothing happens between the moments I type any two letters on the keyboard. As far as the computer is concerned, *this* word is the same as *this* one, even though I took one second to produce the first, and a full minute to produce the second. The machine waits for the next command, and so on, and so on. The time between those commands can be days, or a millisecond.

Because computer code is biased away from continuous time, so too are the programs built on it, and the human behaviors those programs encourage. Everything that we do in the digital realm both benefits and suffers from its occurrence outside time.

Maybe that's why the net's first true "killer app" was email. At first, email did not replace the letter so much as it replaced the phone call. Instead of having to find and catch a real person at home (cell phones were not yet very common), email found a person when he or she wanted to be found. Email was an activity one went and did, usually on a daily or twice-daily basis. (Before and after work, in most cases!)

Unlike the phone, which interrupts our day by unexpectedly ringing whenever someone wants to reach us, email was retrieved when we wanted to see it. And we were free to respond in our own time, on our own conditions. If we didn't have a response at the ready, we could come back later.

The underlying asynchronous quality of email and conferencing was much more obvious to us back then, because we all saw the way these tools really worked. Back then, phone calls still cost money, as did our access time. So our computers generally went online, logged into a server, downloaded everything we were supposed to see, and then logged off again. We did most of our responding while we weren't even online. Then, the next time we went online, our computers would upload the email and posts we had written.

Was it slower? Perhaps. But it was also a more accurate reflection of the way the technologies work, and their bias away from real-time communication. Their strength was never their relationship to the "now," but their ability to slow down or break up the now.

The interactive urge itself—even before computers came into our lives—was consistent with this desire to break time. The first interactive device most of us ever used was the remote control. More than simply allowing us to change channels at the end of a TV program, the remote control gave us the ability to change channels *during* a TV program. The remote control allowed us to deconstruct the narrative of a show, or even a commercial.

Until interactivity, we were defenseless emotional targets for the advertiser, who could use a linear story to put us in a state of vulnerability. Think of almost any television commercial: A person gets in terrible trouble, the product gets her out. A girl gets a pimple before the prom. She tries all sorts of things to get rid of it, making matters worse. Just when it looks like all is lost, she finds the miracle cream. It works, boyfriend shows up, happy prom girl. The continuous narrative arc is used to draw the audience into a state of tension. Only the storyteller—the advertiser—has the way out. To be released from tension, we must accept the storyteller's answer—meaning the advertiser's product. We may have understood that the people making us anxious were not our friends—that the stuff on television is called "programming" for a reason. But we were relatively powerless to do anything about it other than not watch at all.

Before the remote control, the only other way out of imposed anxiety was to get up out of the recliner, take the popcorn off our lap, manually change the channel, and maybe adjust the rabbit ears (an antenna that sat on top of the set for receiving terrestrial broadcast). The amount of effort outweighed the anxiety we were to endure by sitting through the rest of the commercial. But after the remote control, escape from the advertiser's spell becomes effortless. With a micro-motion of the thumb, we are gone. The interactive device introduces discontinuity into an otherwise continuous medium. And this discontinuity—this deconstruction of story—is a form of power.

Likewise, the VCR allowed us to record shows to watch later, and DVR lets us do not only that, but also "pause" shows during broadcast and fast-forward through commercials. Each step of the way, we use the asynchronous bias of digital technology to take control of time. And a medium once celebrated for its ability to "program" the public becomes open to our intervention. Instead of only fostering social programming, the television also fosters a new, postmodern perspective on society's time-honored truths. From Bart Simpson to Stephen Colbert, conventions are turned on their heads.

The spirit of the digital age still finds its expression in this reappropriation of time. Our cutting and pasting, mash-ups and remixes, satires and send-ups all originate in this ability to pause, reflect, and rework.

As Internet connections grow faster, fatter, and freer, however, we are more likely to adopt an "always on" approach to media. Our broadband connections—whether in our homes or in our phones—keep our applications on, updating, and ready at every moment. Anytime anyone or anything wants to message, email, tweet, update, notify, or alert us, something dings on our desktop or vibrates in our pocket. Our devices and, by extension, our nervous systems are now attached to the entire online universe, all the time. Is that my phone vibrating?

We scramble to keep up with the never-ending inflow of demands and commands, under the false premise that moving faster will allow us to get out from under the endless stream of pings for our attention. For answering email and responding to texts or tweets only exacerbates the problem by leading to more responses to our responses, and so on.

We strive to multitask, attempting to give partial attention to more than one thing at a time, when all we really do is move as quickly as possible from one task to another. No matter how proficient we think we are at multitasking, studies show[1] our ability to accomplish tasks accurately and com-

---

1   E. Ophir, C. Nass, and A. D. Wagner. "Cognitive control in media multitaskers." *Proceedings of the National Academy of Sciences* vol. 106 no. 37 (September 2009), 15583–15587.

pletely only diminishes the more we try to do at the same time. This is not the fault of digital technology, but the way we use it.

Instead of our going online to get our email, our email comes to us. Instead of using our inbox as an asynchronous holding bin, we stick it into our phones, which are sure to thump, ding, or shudder with each new incoming message—just to make sure we know something wants our attention. We work against the powerful bias of a timeless technology, and create a situation in which it is impossible to keep up. And so we sacrifice the thoughtfulness and deliberateness our digital media once offered for the false goal of immediacy—as if we really can exist in a state of perpetual standby.

The results aren't pretty. Instead of becoming empowered and aware, we become frazzled and exhausted. We have no time to make considered responses, feeling instead obligated to reply to every incoming message on impulse. We reduce the length and complexity of our responses from paragraphs to sentences to txts, making almost everything we transmit sound like orders barked over a walkie-talkie in a war zone. Everything must happen right away or, better, now. There is no later. This works against the no-time bias of digital media, and so it works against us, even though it might work for the phone company programming the device and inducing our dependence and compliance. (Yes, each variety of beep is studied and tested for its ability to entrain our behavior.)

It's not that the net has somehow changed from an asynchronous medium to a synchronous one. No, it's all still just commands existing in a sequence, outside time. But those commands are coming at us now in increasingly rapid bursts, stimulating us to respond at rates incompatible with human thought and emotion—and in ways that are not terribly enjoyable. Try as we might, we are slow to adapt to the random flood of pings. And our nervous systems are not happy with this arrangement.

For the first time, regular people are beginning to show the signs of stress and mental fatigue once exclusive to air traffic controllers and 911 operators. Cell phone users now complain of "phantom vibration syndrome," the sensation of a cell phone vibrating on your thigh, even though there's no phone in your pocket.

Yet this very discomfort and anxiety compels us to seek still more: The possibility of one great email from a friend, or one good contract offer somewhere down in that list of unanswered messages keeps us compulsively checking our inboxes, iPhones and BlackBerrys like classically conditioned gamblers at the slot machines. And, perhaps counterintuitively, the faster we empty our inbox, the faster it fills up again. Every answered email spawns more. The quicker we respond, the more of an expectation we create that we will respond that rapidly again. An email chain becomes like a conversation happening in real time—except much less efficiently than a phone call. The slower we respond—the more we do the net on our own schedule instead of the one we think it is imposing on us—the more respect we command from the people on the other side of the screen. Unfortunately, many of us don't feel we have even the right to dictate our own relationship to the incoming digital traffic.

Of course, the simplest way out is to refuse to be always on. To engage with the digital—to connect to the network—can still be a choice rather than a given. That's the very definition of autonomy. We can choose to whom or what we want to be available, and when. And we can even choose people for whom we *want* to be always on. Being open to a call from a family member 24/7 doesn't require being open to everyone. The time it takes to program your phone to ring for only certain incoming numbers is trivial compared to the time wasted answering calls from people you don't want to hear from.

We are more likely, however, to ignore the timeless bias of the digital and aspire to catching up with its ever-elusive pace. We mistake the rapid-fire stimulus of our networks for immediacy, and the moment we are actually living in for the thing that needs to catch up. We are like drivers trying to catch up with the image in the rearview mirror.

And the more we live this way, the more we value the digital's definition of the now. Our search engines preface their more relevant results with a section of "live" links to whatever blog comment, social networking message, or tweet has most recently been posted containing the words in our queries. The only weighting that matters is how few seconds have transpired since it was blurted. This in turn encourages us to value the recent over the relevant.

While media critics and concerned educators lament the effects of short messaging on brain capacity, the real influence of our interaction with these programs is not on our neurons as much as our habits and outlook. Yes, thanks to what is known as neuroplasticity, our brains do change depending on what we do. A brain learning on computers ends up wired differently than a brain learning on textbooks. This is nothing new. Brains learning through text are different than ones that learned through oral teaching, too. Likewise, a kid who plays mostly with dolls ends up wired differently than one who builds bridges with blocks.

There's a misplaced anxiety here. Our brains adapt to different situations. Technologies have always changed us. Fire gave us a way to cook meat, essentially pre-digesting food and altering the evolution of both our teeth and digestive tract. Wearing fur allowed us to shed our own. Likewise, text changed the way we process and remember information, and television changed the way our brains relate to three-dimensional space.

Digital media now extends some of these trajectories, while adding a few of its own. The outsourcing of our memory to machines expands the amount of data to which we have access, but degrades our brain's own ability to remember things. Yet this process of offloading our remembered information began with the invention of text, and met with similar critique even back then. We have been consistently using our brains less as hard drives and more as processors—putting our mental resources into active RAM. What's different now, however, is that it's not just lists, dates, and recipes that are being stored for us, but entire processes. The processes we used to use for finding a doctor or a friend, mapping a route, or choosing a restaurant are being replaced by machines that may, in fact, do it better. What we lose in the bargain, however, is not just the ability to remember certain facts, but to call upon certain skills.

We encode a way of doing something and if the computer is capable of accomplishing that task, we never need to know how it happens again. It's a bit like doing arithmetic by algorithm, which most of us learned for calculating square roots and long division. We learn how to push the numbers through a series of rote steps to get our answer, but forget how or why it really works. Now we're having our computers remember those processes, which removes us one step further from whatever is going on. So instead of simply offloading our memory to external hard drives, we're beginning to offload our thinking as well. And thinking is not like a book you can pick up when you want to, in your own time. It is something that's always on. Are we choosing to surrender the ability to do it without digital assistance? If so, are we prepared to remain connected to our networks all the time? What new ability, if any, are we making room for in the process?

It's not the networking of the dendrites in our skulls that matters so much as how effective and happy we are living that way and, in the case of digital media, how purposefully we get ourselves there. Recognizing the biases of the technologies we bring into our lives is really the only way to stay aware of the ways we are changing in order to accommodate them, and to gauge whether we are happy with that arrangement. Rather than accepting each tool's needs as a necessary compromise in our passively technologized lifestyles, we can instead exploit those very same leanings to make ourselves more human.

Our computers live in the ticks of the clock. We live in the big spaces between those ticks, when the time actually passes. By becoming "always on," we surrender time to a technology that knows and needs no such thing.

II. PLACE

Live in Person

Digital networks are decentralized technologies. They work from far away, exchanging intimacy for distance. This makes them terrifically suitable for long-distance communication and activities, but rather awful for engaging with what—or who—is right in front of us. By using a dislocating technology for local connection, we lose our sense of place, as well as our home field advantage.

Where's Gina?

The popular urban high school senior has over five hundred followers on Twitter (most of them real people) reading her every post to find out where the action is tonight. I'm trailing her, along with a youth culture trendspotter, to see what she does on a typical Friday night: how she makes her decisions, and how she communicates them to her ever-growing posse of followers. Gina is a trendsetter, a social leader, and a creature of the moment—in more ways than one.

She's at a club on the Upper East Side, but seems oblivious to the boys and the music. Instead of engaging with those around her, she's scrolling through text messages on her phone, from friends at other parties, bars, and clubs throughout New

York. She needs to know if the event she's at is "the event to be at," or whether something better is happening at that very moment, somewhere else. Sure enough, a blip on display catches her interest, and in what seems like seconds we're in a cab headed for the East Village.

We arrive at a seemingly identical party, but it's the one that Gina has decided is "the place to be" tonight. Instead of turning the phone off and enjoying herself, however, she turns her phone around, activates the camera, and proceeds to take pictures of herself and her friends—instantly uploading them to her Facebook page for the world to see. She does this for about an hour, until a message comes through one of her networks and she's off to the next location for the cycle to begin all over again.

Gina is the girl who is everywhere at once, yet—ultimately—nowhere at all. She is already violating the first command by maintaining an "always on" relationship to her devices and networks. This has in turn fostered her manic, compulsive need to keep tabs on everything everyone else is doing at all times. It has not only removed her from linear time, however, but also from physical place. She relates to her friends through the network, while practically ignoring whomever she is with at the moment. She relates to the places and people she is actually with only insofar as they are suitable for transmission to others in remote locations. The most social girl in her class doesn't really socialize in the real world at all.

While the intent of digital networks was not to disconnect a high school girl from her real world friendships, the bias of the networks were absolutely intended to favor decentralized activity. After all, the net was developed as a communications platform capable of withstanding nuclear attack. Messages—whether text, audio, or video—move through the network as "packets," each taking different routes from node to node until they find their destination. The network is still controlled centrally by an authority (we'll get to this later), but it functions in a decentralized way.

As a result, **digital media are biased away from the local, and toward dislocation**. Just as television is better at broadcasting a soccer game occurring on the other side of the world than it is at broadcasting the pillow talk of the person next to you in bed, the net is better at creating simulations and approximations of human interaction from a great distance than it is at fostering interactions between people in the same place.

For the bias of media has always been toward distance— that's part of what media are for. Text allowed a person in one place (usually a king with a messenger running on foot) to send a message to a person in another place. To those with the power of the written word, what was happening far away became actionable, or even changeable. Similarly, broadcast media gave the newly minted national brands of the industrial age a way to communicate their value across great distances. Where a customer may have once depended on a personal relationship with a local merchant, now he could relate instead to the messaging of a nationally advertised product.

As the promoters of distance over the local, media have also promoted the agendas of long-distance interests over those of people in localities. Sometimes this is a great thing. It allows an entire nation to rally around an issue or idea, forces everyone to notice an injustice that might be happening far away, and even shows how all people are on some level the same. This bias toward non-local thinking can be threatening to parochial interests, and explains much of the origins of resentment for the Judeo-Christian tradition and its text-inspired emphasis on a universal deity and ethics over the local gods and laws of particular regions.

Likewise, big media and the corporations paying them became the enemy of local companies and their workers. Technology and media traditionally worked to make commerce more global, favoring big business over local interests. Mass production distanced workers from the value they were creating. Instead of making a product from beginning to end, each worker on an assembly line completed one small task in the overall process. The product moves from person to person—or even nation to nation—as it is assembled. Each person means less to the production cycle. One's skill level becomes less important as repeatable processes replace craftsmanship and expertise. Workers become cheaper and replaceable, while corporate pricing power puts local companies out of business. Towns become ever more dependent on foreign-owned factories for employment.

Mass-produced products require mass marketing to sell them. Instead of buying oats from Bob the miller, people—now "consumers"—were to purchase them from a big company a thousand miles away in Ohio. The face of a Quaker on the package helped to re-create the kind of bond people used to enjoy with the fellow community members with whom they previously exchanged goods. Finally, a mass media arose to promote these long-distance brand images to an entire nation. Through radio and television, non-local companies could seed a market with their brands and mythologies before the package even made it to the shelf.

Mass media became the non-local brand's way of competing against the people with whom we actually worked and lived. Local businesses competed against both national brands and retail chains for local dollars—and mass media favored mass production and mass marketing over local production and community relationships. The value of transactions became limited to what could be measured in dollars, and ended at the moment of sale. All of the social value of the exchange was lost—and the money itself left the community. This trend reinforced itself as people—embarrassed to have abandoned a local business for the big-box store—began to spend less time on Main Street or at local functions where they might run into local merchants. Local bonds deteriorated, and formerly productive towns turned into bedroom communities of commuters.

While cable television and, now, Internet marketing give smaller businesses a way to peddle their wares in the same media as their corporate counterparts, it may actually work against their real strength as real world, local companies. The power of a local business—or any local enterprise—is its connection to a particular region and people. Its locality is its strength. By turning to a decentralized medium to engage with people right around the corner, a local business loses its home field advantage. Its banner ads will never look as good as those coming out of a marketing agency anyway.

To be sure, one can use the net to organize a local group, schedule a meet-up, or get parents to a school board meeting. But in each of these cases, the non-local bias of the net is accepted as a means to an end: We go online in order to communicate with people who are not with us at that moment, and hopefully to arrange a time and place to meet for real. Further, for people who already know each other well in real life to engage online is very different than engaging with strangers we know only online. The net can reinforce real world relationships when those relationships already exist.

Interactive technology has also allowed for conversations to take place in a media landscape that formerly promoted only one-way broadcast. For those of us living in a world already disconnected by mass marketing and media, these little pings can be very real, and very compelling. A mediaspace that used to make us feel utterly alone now connects us to anyone, anywhere. For some, this means finding other people like themselves for the very first time. Survivors of rare cancers can find support groups, gay kids can find people who have lived through being the only "out" student in a high school, and fans of esoteric books or music can find global communities willing to discuss what no one else in their lives even knows exists.

But those back-and-forth exchanges are occurring at a distance. They are better than nothing—particularly for people in unique situations—but they are not a replacement for real interaction. In fact, the ease with which a simulated, digital connection is made can often make us more distant. The homebound geriatric now has an easy way to connect to her church "virtually" every Sunday morning—and parishioners don't have to worry about who is going to her home to transport her and her wheelchair that week. It takes less effort, but it's also less beneficial for everybody concerned. Giving and accepting kindness used to be part of package.

Similarly, digital technologies can bring news and pictures to us from far away, instantaneously and constantly. We can watch live feed of the oil from an underwater well leaking into the ocean, or a cell phone video of an activist getting murdered in the street by a dictator's police. But with little more to do about it than blog from the safety of our bedrooms, such imagery tends to disconnect and desensitize us rather than engage us fully. Besides, it's "over there" somewhere.

Meanwhile, what is happening just outside our window is devalued. As we come to depend on the net for our sense of connection to each other and the world, we end up fetishizing the tools through which all this happens. We associate our computer screens and email accounts with our most profound experiences of community and connection, and mistake blog comments sections for our most significant conversations.

And so we begin to use long-distance technologies by default, even in local situations where face-to-face contact would be easier. I'll never forget being proudly escorted by a college administrator to a classroom that had been used for a model United Nations for the past ten years. This year, however, they were doing things differently: Instead of having the students re-create the General Assembly in their classroom, they would do it in an online simulation called Second Life. When I got to the room, I saw forty students sitting at desks outfitted with high-resolution computer screens. Although the students were all in the same place at the same time, they were not looking at one another, but at the monitors on their desks. On the monitors was an approximation of a room very much like the one they were in—but without the computers.

A simulation like this might be great for students of an online university to engage more fully with one another, or for students from around the world to experience something like the United Nations without having to travel. But for students and a school who have already spent the time, money, and energy to get to a real classroom at a real college, why throw all that away for a video game version of engagement?

Similarly, I very often find the hosts of my talks flabbergasted when they learn I will be presenting without the aid of a computer slideshow. Some have even been brought to the brink of canceling an event for fear of how their audiences might react to a speaker who presents without computer-generated visuals. What they can't seem to grasp is that I could just as easily deliver a digital slideshow live from the comfort of my home via broadband Internet. There's no need to fly a human body two thousand miles for that. No, the reason to spend the jet fuel to bring a human body across a country or an ocean is for the full-spectrum communication that occurs between human beings in real spaces with one another. The digital slideshow, in most cases, is a distraction—distancing people from one another by mediating their interaction with electronic data.

This misguided tendency to depend on long-distance technology to enhance up-close encounters is completely understandable and forgivable. The more connected we feel in digital spaces, the less securely connected many of us feel in real ones. After days or weeks connecting with people through video chats, the sensation of someone's eyes actually looking into our own in real life can be overwhelming and disorienting.

Similarly, after years of understanding our businesses as brands whose values can be communicated entirely in an ad, it's only natural for us to lose sight of what it means to run an enterprise in a particular place. It's as if the whole notion of place has been surrendered to the digital realm's non-local reality. Wherever you might be, it's just another set of GPS coordinates.

By recognizing digital media's bias for dislocation, we are enabled to exploit its strength delivering interactivity over long distances, while preserving our ability to engage without its interference when we want to connect locally. Many businesses—particularly the biggest ones—already exist in a non-local reality. The entire history of industrial corporatism, from colonial empires to the railroad barons of the nineteenth century, depended on disconnecting people from their local strength and commanding them from afar. For them, it is just as ridiculous to use the net to feign that they are local enterprises as it is for local enterprises to use it to act in the manner of national brands. Powerful global companies become weak local ones, while promising local companies become weak global players.

The digital age offers us all the opportunity to recognize the dislocating bias of our interactive media. With that knowledge, we may choose when we wish to live and work in real places, with one another and—unique to living humans—in person.

III. CHOICE

You May Always Choose
None of the Above

In the digital realm, everything is made into a choice. The medium is biased toward the discrete. This often leaves out things we have not chosen to notice or record, and forces choices when none need to be made.

The difference between an analog record and a digital CD is really quite simple. The record is the artifact of a real event that happened in a particular time and place. A musician plays an instrument while, nearby, a needle cuts a groove in a wax disk (or disturbs the electrons on a magnetic tape). The sound vibrates the needle, leaving a physical record of the noise that can be turned into a mold and copied. When someone else passes a needle over the jagged groove on one of the copies, the original sound emerges. No one has to really know anything about the sound for this to work. It's just a physical event—an impression left in matter.

A CD, on the other hand, is not a physical artifact but a symbolic representation. It's more like text than it is like sound. A computer is programmed to measure various parameters of the sound coming from a musician's instrument. The computer assigns numerical values, many times a second, to the sound in an effort to represent it mathematically. Once the numerical—or "digital"—equivalent of the recording is quantified, it can be transferred to another computer, which then synthesizes the music from scratch based on those numbers.

The analog recording is a physical impression, while the digital recording is a series of choices. The former is as smooth and continuous as real time; the latter is a series of numerical snapshots. The record has as much fidelity as the materials will allow. The CD has as much fidelity as the people programming its creation thought to allow. The numbers used to represent the song—the digital file—is perfect, at least on its own terms. It can be copied exactly, and infinitely.

In the digital recording, however, only the dimensions of the sound that can be measured and represented in numbers are taken into account. Any dimensions that the recording engineers haven't taken into consideration are lost. They are simply not measured, written down, stored, and reproduced. It's not as if they can be rediscovered later on some upgraded playback device. They are gone.

Given how convincingly real a digital recording can seem—especially in comparison with a scratchy record—this loss may seem trivial. After all, if we can't hear it, how important could it be? Most of us have decided it's not so important at all. But early tests of analog recordings compared to digital ones revealed that music played back on a CD format had much less of a positive impact on depressed patients than the same recording played back on a record. Other tests showed that digitally recorded sound moved the air in a room significantly differently than analog recordings played through the same speakers. The bodies in that room would, presumably, also experience that difference—even if we humans can't immediately put a name or metric on exactly what that difference is.

So digital audio engineers go back and increase the sampling rates, look to measure things about the sound they didn't measure before, and try again. If the sampling rate and frequency range are "beyond the capability of the human ear" then it is presumed the problem is solved. But the problem is not that the digital recording is not good enough—it is that it's a fundamentally different phenomenon from the analog one. The analog really just happens—the same way the hands of a clock move slowly around the dial, passing over the digits in one smooth motion. The digital recording is more like a digital clock, making absolute and discrete choices about when those seconds are changing from one to the next.

These choices—these artificially segmented decision points—appear very real to us. They are so commanding, so absolute. Nothing in the real world is so very discrete, however. We can't even decide when life begins and ends, much less when a breath is complete or when the decay of a musical note's echo has truly ended—if it ever does. Every translation of a real thing to the symbolic realm of the digital requires that such decisions be made.

The digital realm is biased toward choice, because everything must be expressed in the terms of a discrete, yes-or-no, symbolic language. This, in turn, often forces choices on humans operating within the digital sphere. We must come to recognize the increased number of choices in our lives as largely a side effect of the digital; we always have the choice of making no choice at all.

All this real and illusory choice—all these unnecessary decision points—may indeed be a dream come true for marketers desperate to convince us that our every consumer preference matters. But it's not their fault. They are merely exploiting digital technology's preexisting bias for yes-or-no decisions.

After all, the very architecture of the digital is numbers; every file, picture, song, movie, program, and operating system is just a number. (Open a video or picture of a loved one in your text editor to see it, if you're interested.) And to the computer, that number is actually represented as a series of 1's and 0's. There's nothing in between that 1 and 0, since a computer or switch is either on or off. All the messy stuff in between yes and no, on and off, just doesn't travel down wires, through chips, or in packets. For something to be digital, it *has* to be expressed in digits.

It's in that translation from the blurry and nondescript real world of people and perceptions to the absolutely defined and numerical world of the digital where something might be lost. Exactly where in the spectrum between yellow and red is that strange shade of orange? 491 terahertz? A little more? 491.5? 0.6? Somewhere in between? How exact is enough? That's anyone's call, but what must be acknowledged first is that someone is, indeed, calling it. A choice is being made.

This isn't a bad thing; it's just how computers work. It's up to the cyborg philosophers of the future to tell us whether everything in reality is just information, reducible to long strings of just two digits. The issue here is that even if our world is made of pure information, we don't yet know enough about that data to record it. We don't know all the information, or how to measure it. For now, our digital representations are compromises—symbol systems that record or transmit a great deal about what matters to us at any given moment. Better digital technology merely makes those choices at increasingly granular levels.

And while our computers are busy making discrete choices about the rather indiscrete and subtle world in which we live, many of us are busy, too—accommodating our computers by living and defining ourselves in their terms. We are making choices not because we want to, but because our programs demand them.

For instance, information online is stored in databases. A database is really just a list—but the computer or program has to be able to be able to parse and use what's inside the list. This means someone—the programmer—must choose what questions will be asked and what options the user will have in responding: Man or Woman? Married or Single? Gay or Straight? It gets very easy to feel left out. Or old: 0–12, 13–19, 20–34, 35–48, or 49–75? The architecture of databases requires the programmer to pick the categories that matter, and at the granularity that matters to his or his employer's purpose.

As users, all we see is a world of choice—and isn't choice good? Here are one hundred possible looks for your mail browser, twenty possible dispositions each with twenty subsets for you to define yourself on a dating site, one hundred options for you to configure your car, life insurance, or sneaker. When it doesn't feel overwhelming, it feels pretty empowering—at least for a while. More choice is a good thing, right? We equate it with more freedom, autonomy, self-determination, and democracy.

But it turns out more choice doesn't really do all this. We all want the freedom to choose, and the history of technology can easily be told as the story of how human beings gave themselves more choices: the choice to live in different climates, to spend our time doing things other than hunting for food, to read at night, and so on. Still, there's a value set attending all this choice, and the one choice we're not getting to make is whether or not to deal with all this choice.

Choice stops us, requiring that we make a decision in order to move on. Choice means selecting one option while letting all the others go. Imagine having to choose your college major before taking a single course. Each option passed over is an opportunity cost—both real and imagined. The more choices we make (or are forced to make) the more we believe our expectations will be met. But in actual experience, our pursuit of choice has the effect of making us less engaged, more obsessive, less free, and more controlled. And forced choice is no choice at all, whether for a hostage forced to choose which of her children can survive, or a social network user forced to tell the world whether she is married or single.

Digital technology's bias toward forced choices dovetails all too neatly with our roles as consumers, reinforcing this notion of choice as somehow liberating while turning our interactive lives into fodder for consumer research. Websites and programs become laboratories where our keystrokes and mouse clicks are measured and compared, our every choice registered for its ability to predict and influence the next choice.

The more we accept each approximation as accurate, the more we reinforce these techniques from our machines and their programmers. Whether it's an online bookstore suggesting books based on our previous selections (and those of thousands of other consumers with similar choice histories), or a consumer research firm using kids' social networking behaviors to predict which ones will someday self-identify as gay (yes, they can do that now), choice is less about giving people what they want than getting them to take what the choice-giver has to sell.

Meanwhile, the more we learn to conform to the available choices, the more predictable and machinelike we become ourselves. We train ourselves to stay between the lines, like an image dragged onto a "snap-to" grid: It never stays quite where we put it, but jerks up and over to the closest available place on the predetermined map.

Likewise, through our series of choices about the news we read, feeds to which we subscribe, and websites we visit, we create a choice filter around ourselves. Friends and feeds we may have chosen arbitrarily or because we were forced to in the past soon become the markers through which our programs and search engines choose what to show us next. Our choices narrow our world, as the infinity of possibility is lost in the translation to binary code.

One emerging alternative to forced, top-down choice in the digital realm is "tagging." Instead of a picture, blog entry, or anything being entirely defined by its predetermined category, users who come upon it are free (but not obligated) to label it themselves with a tag. The more people who tag it a certain way, the more easily others looking for something with that tag will find it. While traditional databases are not biased toward categorizing things in an open-ended, bottom-up fashion, they are capable of operating this way. They needn't be limited by the original choices programmed into them but can be programmed instead to expand their dimensions and categories based on the tags and preferences of the people using them. They can be made to conform to the way people think, instead of demanding we think like they do. It's all in the programming, and in our awareness of how these technologies will be biased if we do not intervene consciously in their implementation.

Meanwhile, we are always free to withhold choice, resist categorization, or even go for something not on the list of available options. You may always choose none of the above. Withholding choice is not death. Quite on the contrary, it is one of the few things distinguishing life from its digital imitators.

IV. COMPLEXITY

You Are Never Completely Right

Although they allowed us to work with certain kinds of complexity in the first place, our digital tools often oversimplify nuanced problems. Biased against contradiction and compromise, our digital media tend to polarize us into opposing camps, incapable of recognizing shared values or dealing with paradox. On the net, we cast out for answers through simple search terms rather than diving into an inquiry and following extended lines of logic. We lose sight of the fact that our digital tools are modeling reality, not substituting for it, and mistake its oversimplified contours for the way things should be. By acknowledging the bias of the digital toward a reduction of complexity, we regain the ability to treat its simulations as models occurring in a vacuum rather than accurate depictions of our world.

Thanks to its first three biases, digital technology encourages us to make decisions, make them in a hurry, and make them about things we've never seen for ourselves up close. Furthermore, because these choices must all be expressed in numbers, they are only accurate to the nearest decimal place. They are approximations by necessity. But they are also absolute: At the end of the day, digital technologies are saying either yes or no.

This makes digital technology—and those of us using it—biased toward a reduction of complexity.

For instance, although reality is more than one level deep, most of our digital networks are accessible with a single web search. All knowledge is the same distance away—just once removed from where we are now. Instead of pursuing a line of inquiry, treading a well-worn path or striking out on an entirely new one, we put a search term in a box and get back more results than we can possibly read. The pursuit itself is minimized—turned into a one-dimensional call to our networks for a response.

On the one hand, this is tremendously democratizing. The more accessible information becomes in a digital age, the less arbitrary its keepers can be about who they let in, and who is kept out. Many playing fields are leveled as regular people gain access to information formerly available only to doctors, physicists, defense contractors, or academics.

It's not just that the data is in unrestricted places—it's that one no longer needs to know quite how to find it. The acquisition of knowledge used to mean pursuing a prescribed path and then getting to the knowledge desired when the path reached there. The seeker had to jump through the hoops left by his predecessors. Now, the seeker can just get the answer.

And in some cases—many cases even—this is a terrific thing. A cancer patient doesn't need ten years of medical training to read about a particular course of chemotherapy, a citizen doesn't need a law degree to study how a new tax code might affect his business, a student doesn't need to read all of *Romeo and Juliet* to be able to answer questions about it on a test. (Well, at least it feels like a great thing at the time.) We only get into trouble if we equate such cherry-picked knowledge with the kind one gets pursuing a genuine inquiry.

In today's harried net culture, actually sitting down to read an entire Wikipedia article on a subject—especially after we've found the single fact we need—seems like a luxury. We hardly remember how embarrassing (and failing) it was to be discovered to have used an encyclopedia article as the source in a paper as early as middle school. It's not just that teachers considered using encyclopedias and plot summaries cheating. Rather, it was generally understood that these watered-down digests of knowledge deny a person the learning that takes place along the way. Actually reading the scenes in a Shakespeare play, or following the process through which Mendel inferred genetics from the variations in his garden pea plants, promotes experiential learning. It re-creates the process of discovery, putting the researcher through the very motion of cognition rather than simply delivering the bounty.

Is this an old-fashioned way of acquiring knowledge? Indeed it is. And it's not essential for every single fact we might need. Figuring out the sales tax rate in Tennessee needn't require us to revisit the evolution of the state's tax code. Thank heavens there's an Internet making such information a single search away.

But not everything is a data point. Yes, thanks to the digital archive we can retrieve any piece of data on our own terms, but we do so at the risk of losing its context. Our knee-jerk, digital age reaction against academic disciplines finds its footing in our resentment for centuries of repressive hierarchies. Professors, gurus, and pundits made us pay for access to their knowledge, in one way or another. Still, although they may have abused their monopolies, some of the journeys on which they sent us were valid. The academic disciplines were developed over centuries, as each new era of experts added to and edited the body of what they considered to be essential knowledge. By abandoning the disciplines—however arbitrarily they may have been formulated—we disconnect ourselves from the multigenerational journey leading up to this moment. We are no longer part of that bigger project, or even know what it is we are rejecting.

In the more immediate sense, facts devoid of context are almost impossible to apply sensibly. They become the fodder for falsely constructed arguments of one side or other of the social or political spectrum. The single vote of a politician is used to describe his entire record, a single positive attribute of caffeine or tobacco receives attention thanks to public relations funding, and a picture of a single wounded child turns public opinion against one side in a conflict rather than against war itself.

Both sides in a debate can cherry-pick the facts that suit them—enraging their constituencies and polarizing everybody. In a digital culture that values data points over context, everyone comes to believe they have the real answer and that the other side is crazy or evil. Once they reach this point, it no longer matters that the opposing side's facts contradict one's own: True believers push through to a new level of cynicism where if the facts are contradictory, it means they are all irrelevant. The abundance of facts ends up reducing their value to us.

As a result, we tend to retreat into tribes, guided primarily by our uninformed rage. And we naturally hunger for reinforcement. Television news shows rise to the occasion, offering shouting matches between caricatured opposites competing for ratings. Elected officials are ridiculed as "wonks" for sharing or even understanding multiple viewpoints, the history of an issue, or its greater context. We forget that these are the people we're paying to learn about these issues on our behalf. Instead, we overvalue our own opinions on issues about which we are ill informed, and undervalue those who are telling us things that are actually more complex than they look on the surface. They become the despised "elite."

Appropriately used, however, the data-point universe can yield uniquely valuable connections and insights. Thousands or millions of amateurs, working through problems together or independently, can link to one another's results and sources. Instead of depending on a top-down academic discipline (which may be more committed to the preservation of old heroes than the solving of new problems), researchers can discern which sources are most valuable to their peers right now. Information can be structured and restructured in real time, catered to new challenges unforeseen by yesterday's academics. Physics and biology no longer need to live in different departments of the university, and James Joyce can appear on the same virtual library shelf as a text on chaos math. In a hypertext-driven information space, everybody's library can look different every day.

To exploit the power of these new arrangements of data, we must learn to regard them as what they are: untested models, whose relevancy is at best conditional or even personal. This is your brain's way of organizing some pieces of information for a very particular task. It is not a substitute for knowledge of that realm. It is just a new entry point. Which is not to suggest this way of approaching information isn't quite novel or even powerful.

Young people, in particular, are developing the ability to get the gist of an entire area of study with just a moment of interaction with it. With a channel surfer's skill, they are able to experience a book, movie, or even a scientific process almost intuitively. For them, hearing a few lines of T. S. Eliot, seeing one geometric proof, or looking at a picture of an African mask leaves them with a real, albeit oversimplified, impression of the world from which it comes. This works especially well for areas of art and study that are "fractal" or holographic in nature, where one tiny piece reflects the essence of the whole.

By recognizing that our engagements through and with the digital world tend to reduce the complexity of our real world, we lessen the risk of equating these oversimplified impressions with real knowledge and experience. The digital information gatherer tends to have the opposite approach to knowledge as his text-based ancestors, who saw research as an excuse to sit and read old books. Instead, net research is more about engaging with data in order to dismiss it and move on— like a magazine one flips through not to read, but to make sure there's nothing that *has* to be read. Reading becomes a process of elimination rather than deep engagement. Life becomes about knowing how *not* to know what one doesn't *have* to know.

Ironically, perhaps, as our digital experiences make us more simple, our machines are only getting more complex. The more complex our technologies become, and more impenetrable their decision-making (especially by our increasingly simplified, gist-of-it brains), the more dependent on them we become. Their very complexity becomes the new anxiety, replacing the adman's storytelling as the predominant form of social influence. While digital technology liberated us from our roles as passive spectators of media, their simplifying bias reduced us once again to passive spectators of technology itself. For most of us, the announcement of the next great "iThing" provokes not eagerness but anxiety: Is this something else we will have to pay for and learn to use? Do we even have a choice?

With each upgrade in technology, our experience of the world is further reduced in complexity. The more advanced and predictive the smart-phone interface, the less a person needs to know to use it—or how it even makes its decisions. Instead of learning about our technology, we opt for a world in which our technology learns about *us*. It's our servant, after all, so why shouldn't it just do what it knows we want and deliver it however it can? Because the less we know about how it works, the more likely we are to accept its simplified models as reality. Its restaurant recommendations substitute for our personal knowledge of our neighborhood; its talking maps substitute for our knowledge of our roads (as well as the logic or lack of logic in their design); its green or red stock tickers substitute for our experience of wealth and well-being.

Again, this is only a problem if we mistake our digital models for reality. Restaurant recommendations, mapping functions, and stock tickers are ways of understanding worlds—not the worlds themselves. But the latest research into virtual worlds suggests that the lines between the two may be blurring. A Stanford scientist testing kids' memories of virtual reality experiences has found that at least half of children cannot distinguish between what they really did and what they did in the computer simulation.[2] Two weeks after donning headsets and swimming with virtual whales, half of the participants interviewed believed they had actually had the real-world experience. Likewise, Philip Rosedale—the quite sane founder of the virtual reality community Second Life—told me he believes that by 2020, his online world will be indistinguishable from real life.

I doubt there's a computer simulation on the horizon capable of accurately representing all the activity in a single cubic centimeter of soil or the entire sensory experience of clipping one toenail, much less an entire social world of thousands of human users. But even if such a prediction were true, our inability to distinguish between a virtual reality simulation and the real world will have less to do with the increasing fidelity of simulation than the decreasing perceptual abilities of us humans. As we know even personally, our time spent looking into screens harms our eyesight, wearing earbuds harms our hearing, and crouching over a keyboard harms our ability to move.

Digital simulations also have their own effect on our perceptual apparatus. The sound-file format used in most digital music players, MP3, is really just an algorithm. The MP3 algorithm takes digital audio files (themselves just

---

2. See my interview with Jeremy Bailenson in the *Frontline* documentary *Digital Nation* at www.frontline.org, or read Jeremy Bailenson and Kathryn Y. Segovia, "Virtual Doppelgangers: Psychological Effects of Avatars Who Ignore Their Owners," in W.S. Bainbridge (ed.), *Online Worlds: Convergence of the Real and the Virtual*, Human-Computer Interaction Series (London: Springer-Verlag, 2010), 175. (http://vhil.stanford.edu/pubs/2010/bailenson-ow-virtual-doppelgangers.pdf).

numbers) and reduces them even further to save space. The algorithm was developed to simulate the main features of sound that reverberate in people's ears. The MP3 algorithm has a way of creating the sensation of bass, the sensation of high notes, and so on. Listening to these files in lieu of music, however, seems to strain or even retrain our hearing. As new and disturbing studies in Germany have shown,[3] young people raised on MP3s can no longer distinguish between the several hundred thousand musical sounds their parents can hear.

This shouldn't diminish the brilliance and importance of these simulation technologies, or the many ways computer scientists have learned to approximate reality through them. While they are poor substitutes for the full spectrum of nature, they are great models for particular systems that we would have no way to isolate from their contexts in the real world. A weather system can be studied purely in terms of pressure zones, a financial market can be analyzed through the axes of supply and demand, and a digital map can represent the world in terms of wealth, violence, or real-time births.

Because digital simulations are numerical models, many choices about them must be made in advance. Models are necessarily reductive. They are limited by design. This does not negate their usefulness; it merely qualifies it. Digital reduction yields maps. These maps are great for charting a course, but they are not capable of providing the journey. No matter how detailed or interactive the map gets, it cannot replace the territory.

---

3. See Todd Oppenheimer, *The Flickering Mind: The False Promise of Technology* (New York: Random House, 2003).

V. SCALE

One Size Does Not Fit All

On the net, everything scales—or at least it's supposed to. Digital technologies are biased toward abstraction, bringing everything up and out to the same universal level. People, ideas, and businesses that don't function on that level are disadvantaged, while those committed to increasing levels of abstraction tend to dominate. By remembering that one size does not fit all, we can preserve local and particular activities in the face of demands to scale up.

Tom, the owner of a small music shop in upstate New York, decided it was time for him to finally get his business online. He hired a local college student to build him a website, complete with a shopping cart and checkout. He soon discovered that his online transactions were less expensive than the ones he did in real life. For web customers, he didn't have to maintain a physical store—and didn't even have to purchase stock or pay shipping. One of the big delivery companies took care of fulfillment, and sent orders directly from the manufacturers to Tom's customers.

Tom began encouraging his walk-in customers to use the site, going so far as to put a laptop on the counter of the store. After a few months, he gave up the physical shop altogether and—at the advice of supposedly net-savvy friends like me—Tom spent his time writing a music blog to characterize his business and share his expertise online.

Along came "shopping aggregators"—programs that sweep through the net for the best prices on any product—and there went Tom's margins. His prices were good, but he couldn't compete with the chain stores. When his offerings showed up in the same list as the other stores but just a couple of dollars higher, even his loyal customers went elsewhere. People still read his blog, but bought from his cheaper, bigger competitors. The fact that he was no longer a live human interacting face-to-face with another community member didn't help matters. What's the difference between one web page and another, anyway? It's all in the same browser window.

Tom's error wasn't just that he closed down his sustainable local business; it was that he couldn't scale. **On the net, everything is occurring on the same abstracted and universal level. Survival in a purely digital realm—particularly in business—means being able to scale, and winning means being able to move up one level of abstraction beyond everyone else.** The music retailers that could scale effectively survived the net; the companies that went up a level and aggregated those music retailers triumphed.

The net has turned scalability from a business option to a business requirement. Real world companies have always generally had the choice of whether they want to remain at the "mom and pop" level, or to become a chain or franchise—essentially going into the business of business. Beginning the 1970s, shopping malls and big-box stores changed the retail landscape, putting the pressure of internationally scaled competition onto local businesses. By the 1990s, migrating to the net seemed to many like a way to fight back: No website seemed to be intrinsically advantaged over another. Now the smallest players could have the same reach as the big boys.

But as Tom learned, going online also denied him his remaining competitive advantage, the human relationships and local connections he enjoyed in the real world. Instead, going online forced him into the electronic mall itself—a place where he was no longer capable of competing on any level. Even his store's blog and recommendations were consumed as if they were completely disconnected from his own stock and cash register. The fact that his insights could be searched and retrieved by content aggregators didn't help keep his expertise associated with his own merchandise.

Because the net is occurring on a single, oversimplified and generic level, success has less to do with finding a niche than establishing a "vertical" or a "horizontal." Going vertical means establishing oneself as the place to do everything in a particular industry: the one-stop place for hardware, or cycling needs, or home electronics. Going horizontal means to offer a service that applies to every category's transactions, like the company that made the credit card transaction software for Tom's music website. In either case, "scaling up" means cutting through the entire cloud in one direction or another: becoming all things to some people, or some things to all people.

The craftiest online businesspeople have come to realize that neither of those strategies is perfect. Both vertical and horizontal businesses face competition from their peers in an increasingly commodified landscape. It's almost impossible to establish a foothold that can't get undercut by a tiny shift in the price of one component. So instead of going into business, these players become search engines, portals, or aggregators, rising one level above all those competing businesses and skimming profit off the top. In an abstracted universe where everything is floating up in the same cloud, it is the indexer who provides context and direction.

Of course, this logic dovetails perfectly with a financial industry in which derivatives on transactions matter more than the transactions themselves. Once the financial world came to understand that its own medium—central currency—was biased in the interests of the lender and not the producer, every business attempted to get out of the business it was actually in, and scale up to become a holding company. Thus, great industrial companies like General Electric shed their factories and got involved in capital leasing, banking, and commercial credit. Meanwhile, those who were already in banking and credit moved up one level of abstraction as well, opening hedge funds and creating derivatives instruments that won or lost money based on the movements of economic activity occurring one level below. Even craftier speculators began writing derivatives of derivatives, and so on, and so on.

The existing bias of business toward abstraction combined with the net's new emphasis on success through scale yielded a digital economy with almost no basis in actual commerce, the laws of supply and demand, or the creation of value. It's not capitalism in the traditional sense, but an abstracted hyper-capitalism utterly divorced from getting anything done. In fact, the closer to the creation of value you get under this scheme, the farther you are from the money.

But new theories of net economics abounded, each one depending on another misapplied principle from chaos math, systems theory, or even biology. The emergent behavior of slime mold becomes the justification for the consciousness of the market and fractal geometry is misused to prove that the economic behavior occurring on one level of society is mirrored on all the others. All of these new perspectives relied on the very same digitally determined axiom that everything can and should be abstracted from everything else.

What all this abstraction does accomplish here on earth, however, is make everyone and everything more dependent on highly centralized standards. Instead of granting power to small businesses on the periphery, the net ends up granting even more authority to the central authorities, indexers, aggregators, and currencies through which all activity must pass. Without the search engine, we are lost. Without centrally directed domain name servers, the search engines are lost. Further, since digital content itself needs to be coded and decoded, it requires tremendous standardization from the outset. Far from liberating people and their ideas from hierarchies, the digital realm enforces central control on an entirely new level.

On a more subtle level, the abstraction intrinsic to the digital universe makes us rely more heavily on familiar brands and trusted authorities to gain our bearings. Like tourists in a foreign city sighing in relief at the sight of a Starbucks or American Express sign, users tend to depend more on centrally defined themes and instantly recognizable brands. They are like signposts, even for the young people we consider digital natives, who turn out to be even more reliant on brand names and accepted standards for understanding and orientation than are their digital immigrant counterparts. Activism means finding a website, joining a movement, or "liking" a cause—all of which exist on a plane above and beyond their human members. Learning, orienting, and belonging online depend on universally accepted symbols or generically accessible institutions.

Likewise, achievement is equated with becoming one of those universal symbols oneself. The digitally oriented activist is no longer satisfied with making something real happen where she lives but, rather, dedicated to building the website that solves the problem for everyone. Everyone wants to have his or her model of change scale up, to host the website where the most important conversation takes place, or aggregate the Twitter feeds of all the people one level below.

This tendency is only natural when working on a platform *biased* toward abstraction.

In fact, all media are biased toward abstraction in one way or another. By allowing us to describe events that had already taken place or those that had happened to other people, speech disconnected the doer from the deed. Text, meanwhile, disconnected speech from the speaker. Print disconnected text from the scribe, and the computer disconnected print from paper. At each level of disconnection, these media became more abstract.

Language is an abstraction of the real world, where sounds represent things and actions. It requires a tremendous amount of agreement, so that the same words mean the same thing to different people. Text is an abstraction of those sounds—with little squiggly lines now representing the mouth noises that compose the words that represent real stuff. Over time, the way those letters look is standardized so that the written language becomes increasingly universal and applicable.

Of course, the written word separates the speaker from his words. A person can put his words down on paper and be gone by the time it is read. He is at once more accountable for having written down his message or promise, and less accountable for not having to be there in the flesh with the reader. It is easier to lie. On the other hand, text is more durable. It creates a record, a standard, and something to refer back to later. The invention of text allowed for contracts, the law, codes of ethics, and even the Bible—a written agreement or "covenant" between people and their new, highly abstracted God. In fact, the God of this new text-based civilization achieved all creation through spoken words.

The printing press standardized text, depersonalizing the writing process, disconnecting the author from the page itself, but allowing for books to "scale" to mass consumption. Thanks to printing, the single author can reach everyone—even though neither he nor the ink from his pen come into contact with them.

Finally, the digital age brings us hypertext—the ability for any piece of writing to be disconnected not just from its author but from its original context. Each link we encounter allows us to exit from a document at any point and, more importantly, offers us access to the bits and pieces of anyone's text that might matter at that moment. In a universe of words where the laws of hypertext are truly in effect, anything can link to anything else. Or, in other words, everything is everything—the ultimate abstraction.

Of course this can be beautiful and even inspiring. The entirety of human thought becomes a hologram, where any piece might reflect on any other, or even recapitulate its entirety. From a Taoist perspective, perhaps this is true. But from a practical and experiential perspective, we are not talking about the real world being so very connected and self-referential, but a world of symbols about symbols. Our mediating technologies do connect us, but on increasingly abstracted levels.

Walter Benjamin, a German philosopher of the early twentieth century, wrote a seminal essay about the way photography and other reproduction technologies change our relationship to art. His observation was that the preponderance of photographs of a work of art in a mass-produced book have a strange effect on the original: While they are themselves utterly divorced from the context in which the original artwork exists, they actually make the original work more sacred. The original painting, hanging in the very cathedral for which it was painted perhaps, has what Benjamin called an "aura," which is at least partly dependent on its context and location. A tourist, having seen its image again and again in books, might travel thousands of miles to encounter the real painting in its home setting and soak in the aura with which it is imbued.

On the other hand, the reproduction is a rather profane imitation, existing in the more abstract and commercial world of mass-produced goods and mass culture. It's not that Benjamin despises popular culture—it's that he sees real art and artifacts being absorbed by a bigger spectacle, and audiences losing the ability and desire to tell the difference between that spectacle and real world.

Strangely enough, as we migrate from his world of mass-produced objects to the realm of even more highly abstracted digital facsimiles, we nostalgically collect the artifacts of midcentury mass production as if they were works of art. Each Philco radio, Heywood Wakefield dresser, or Chambers stove is treasured as if it were an original. We can only wonder if cloud computing may make us nostalgic one day for having a real "file" on the hard drive of one's own computer—or if silicon brain implants may make us wax poetic for the days when one's computing happened on a laptop. In the march toward increasing abstraction, whatever we had previously will seem like the real thing.

By recognizing the abstracting bias of digital technologies, however, we can use it to our advantage. The same way Benjamin would have the printed art book inspire us to visit the original work in its real world context, our digital abstractions work best when they are used to give us insight into something quite real and particular.

In just one example, consider the impact of fantasy baseball on the real game. Fantasy baseball—first developed on an IBM computer in the 1960s—is a game where a participant's roster of baseball players score points based on their statistics over a real baseball season. It's a truly "derivative" game, in that fans create their own fantasy rosters of players, irrespective of their real teams, and in that winning and losing in the fantasy game is on a level fully abstracted from the baseball happening in the real world. Like any digital simulation, the experience of fantasy baseball is empowering to its participants. In fact, the game only became a mass phenomenon as free agenting and Major League players' strikes soured fans on the sport. As baseball became a business, the fans took back baseball as a game—even if it had to happen on their computers.

The effects didn't stay in the computer. Leveraging the tremendous power of digital abstraction back to the real world, Billy Bean, coach of the Oakland Athletics, applied these same sorts of statistical modeling to players for another purpose: to assemble a roster for his own Major League team. Bean didn't have the same salary budget as his counterparts in New York or Los Angeles, and he needed to find another way to assemble a winning combination. So he abstracted and modeled available players in order to build a better team that went from the bottom to the top of its division, and undermined the way that money had come to control the game. Since that time, many fantasy baseball players and digital statisticians have been hired to run the front offices of Major League teams.[*]

So while the dangers of living and working in an inherently abstracted environment are very real, so too are the benefits. Abstraction has been around since language, perhaps even before. Money, math, theology, and games would all be impossible without abstracted symbol systems, accepted standards, and some measure of central authority. The digital realm is no different in that regard.

Yet digital abstraction does occur still one further level removed from what we think of as reality. While games and math might be abstracted representations of our world, our digital simulations are abstracted representations of those games and mathematics. In a world as filled with representations as ours, it is easy to get so entranced by signs that we lose sight of the here and now. As the postmodernists would

---

* Hopefully, my former New School media studies student Jake Kalos will write a book on this, the subject of his excellent unpublished paper.

remind us, we have stuff, we have signs for stuff, and we have symbols of signs. What these philosophers feared was that as we came to live in a world defined more by symbols, we would lose touch altogether with the real stuff; we would become entranced by our simulated reality, and disconnect from the people and places we should care about.

As we watch people wearing headphones and staring into smart phones, ensconced in their private digital bubbles as they walk down what were once public streets, it is hard not to agree with those pessimistic assessments of our procession into simulation.

What the postmodernists may have underestimated, however, was the degree to which the tools through which these symbolic worlds are created—and ways in which they might be applied—would remain accessible to all of us. And how willing we may still be to use them. Just as the framers of the Constitution and the Talmudic scribes before them understood, abstract codes of laws are fine—so long as we're the ones writing them.

VI. IDENTITY

Be Yourself

Our digital experiences are out-of-body. This biases us toward depersonalized behavior in an environment where one's identity can be a liability. But the more anonymously we engage with others, the less we experience the human repercussions of what we say and do. By resisting the temptation to engage from the apparent safety of anonymity, we remain accountable and present—and much more likely to bring our humanity with us into the digital realm.

When signing onto the WELL, an early, dial-in digital bulletin board based in the Bay Area, participants were welcomed with the statement: You Own Your Own Words. To most people, this meant a confirmation of copyright—that everything we posted on the bulletin boards belonged to us, and couldn't be published by someone else without permission. To others, including me, You Own Your Own Words served as an ethical foundation: You, the human being on the other side of the modem, are responsible for what you say and do here. You are accountable.

Given that the WELL was developed by farsighted cultural pioneers such as Stewart Brand, Larry Brilliant, Kevin

Kelly, and Howard Rheingold, we shouldn't be surprised that they sought to compensate for some of the disconnection online between people and their words. And that's why, from the very beginning, I decided to be myself online. I've only used one name on the Internet: Rushkoff. I figured the only real danger was from government, corporations, or some other "big brother" out there using what I posted against me in some future McCarthy hearings. Even if that was the case, if a whole lot of us got in the habit of standing behind everything we said, it would be hard for anyone to get prosecuted or persecuted for what they said or believed. This is America, after all.

Turns out my staunch approach to identity online hadn't made me vulnerable to the authorities so much as to the anonymous—or, as they like to call themselves, Anonymous.

Just last year, I wrote an article defending the existence of a notorious bulletin board where young hackers often congregated and organized against companies and organizations they believed were preventing free speech online—or were simply being evil in one way or another. Sometimes they did creative pranks, like replacing video footage, and other times they simply crashed websites by creating programs that overtaxed the enemies' servers. After a misunderstanding with their own Internet provider, the site was shut down for a short time. An online war ensued, and many authorities and journalists called for the BBS to be shut down. I lurked on the site for a month or so, ended up seeing some particularly raunchy and even illegal stuff, but wrote a piece defending its existence. They are an unwieldy bunch, but sometimes it's reassuring to know that there's still a wild, uncontrollable side to the Internet.

Well, the online magazine for which I wrote the piece framed it a bit too sensationally (another product of digital biases and the desperate quest for "page views"), and the kids on the BBS decided I had written a hit piece. Minutes after my piece was posted, they decided I needed to be taken down. It was as if I had poked at a hornets' nest: It didn't matter what my intentions were, the hive had been provoked. And so dozens of anonymous young hackers went at me—posting every personal fact they could find, crashing my website and the website of the online magazine, making automated phone calls to phone numbers associated with me, and so on. Although most of the information, photos, and phone numbers they posted were inaccurate, a whole lot of people ended up having photos of their homes and private numbers posted online. It wasn't pretty. The anonymous attackers demanded the piece be removed. Not that this would end their assault, but it might turn their main attention elsewhere.

How could a group purportedly dedicated to free speech online end up forcibly censoring an essay defending their free speech in the first place? By operating anonymously.

In a hostile, depersonalized net environment, identity is one's liability. What were the kids' weapons against me? My name, my address, my home. What does putting a picture of someone's house online really imply, after all? We know where you live. We can get you, the real you—while you have no idea who *we* are.

But more than simply protecting them from retribution, the anonymous status of people in an online group engenders crowd behavior. They have nothing to fear as individuals, and get used to taking actions from a distance and from secrecy. As a result, they exacerbate digital technology's most dehumanizing tendencies, and end up behaving angrily, destructively, and automatically. They go from being people to being a mob.

The way to dampen the effects of this problem is not to retreat into anonymity ourselves, but to make being real and identifiable the norm. As in the real world, the fewer people who know each other, the more dangerous the neighborhood.

Of course we should all keep our bank accounts and personal information private; but our posts, our participation, and socializing? That really should be coming from us, ourselves. **The less we take responsibility for what we say and do online, the more likely we are to behave in ways that reflect our worst natures—or even the worst natures of others. Because digital technology is biased toward depersonalization, we must make an effort not to operate anonymously, unless absolutely necessary. We must be ourselves.**

There are certainly instances where anonymity should be maintained. Dissidents in Iran, for example, can be killed for what they say. While posting anonymously confirms the apparent authority of the government to censor through execution, it can also help keep an activist alive. But of course there is also great political power in standing up for what one believes in and hoping many others join in. Every openly gay person makes it easier for the rest of us to be open about our sexuality as well—to be more who we are, not less. Likewise, the millions of people protesting peacefully in the streets of Eastern European dictatorships were masses of individuals, not anonymous mobs. Their identities and collective personhood were their power.

Digital technology allows for similar collective activity—but it is not biased that way. Our digital activity occurs out of body. Whether sending an email, typing a comment to a blog post, or controlling an avatar in a video game, we are not in the computer, at a discussion, or in the fantasy world with our friends. We are at home or the office, behind a computer terminal or game console. We are operating out of our bodies and free of our identities.

This can promote an illusion that we may act without personal consequences. If we choose to maintain our anonymity as well, we are more likely to lash out from the seeming safety of obscurity. As website moderators well understand by now, the more anonymously people are allowed to post to a forum, the more quickly conversations will devolve into "flame wars" or just plain abuse. Requiring that people register to make comments invariably raises the level of conversation as well as the level of civility.

This isn't just because being identifiable means the user can be traced and caught. While the notion of repercussions may dampen the most aberrant or illegal behavior, it alone isn't enough to explain how differently people act when they have an identity. In fact, the civilizing effect is nearly as powerful even when the identity of the user has been created for the specific online environment. For instance, when a gamer has been working with the same character over a period of months, he comes to care about that character as an extension of himself. Even if his real world identity has never been associated with the character, his real world time has been invested in making the character a member of the community. The player has something at stake. Similarly, many bulletin boards award reputation points to users whose posts have been deemed valuable by other members. These points can take years to acquire. Like an eBay "seller rating," the more time it has taken to acquire a reputation in an online environment, the more it matters—even when it is entirely out of body.

Of course, the original hope of virtual community enthusiasts was that the disembodied nature of online interaction might help people overcome long-held prejudices. People couldn't actually see one another, so they often made assumptions about the race, age, gender, and education of other participants. Professors got into extended dialogues with strangers online—who turned out to be laypeople or teenagers, while people of color were treated as equals in business communities for the first time. Such anecdotes are encouraging, for sure, but they may represent less a triumph over prejudice than a detour around it. We are treating the stranger as an equal because we have made the false assumption she is just like us. It's not that we see through our prejudices; we simply don't see the person.

Our experience online is less that of the unprejudiced intellectual than that of the autistic living with Asperger's syndrome. While a lot has been argued back and forth about whether computer use or gaming might cause spectrum disorders, direct observation alone has revealed that our digital behaviors closely mirror those of Asperger's sufferers: a dependence on the verbal over the visual, low pickup on social cues and facial expressions, apparent lack of empathy, and the inability to make eye contact. This describes any of us online, typing to one another, commonly misunderstanding each other's messages, insulting one another unintentionally, or seeking fruitlessly to interpret someone's real meaning by parsing his words repeatedly.

According to best estimates,[4] only 7 percent of human communication occurs on the verbal level. Pitch, volume, and other vocal tone account for 38 percent, and body movements such as gestures and facial expression account for a whopping 55 percent. As we have all experienced, the way a person makes eye contact can mean a whole lot more to us than whatever he is saying.

But online, we are depending entirely on that tiny 7 percent of what we use in the real world. Absent the cues on which we usually depend to feel safe, establish rapport, or show agreement, we are left to wonder what the person on the other end really means or really thinks of us. Our mirror neurons—the parts of our brains that enjoy and are reinforced by seeing someone nod or smile while we are sharing something—remain mute. The dopamine we expect to be released when someone agrees with us doesn't flow. We remain in the suspicious, protective crouch, even when the situation would warrant otherwise—if only we were actually there. Imagine living in a world where you were deaf, dumb, and blind, and had to rely on the text coming at you in order to figure out what people meant and how they felt about you. Then, to this add not knowing who any of the other people really are.

---

4. Mele Koneya and Alton Barbour, *Louder Than Words: Nonverbal Communication*, Interpersonal Communication series, (Columbus, Ohio: Merrill, 1976).

Living in a 7 percent social reality has real effects. As MIT researcher Sherry Turkle has discovered,[5] teens online rarely if ever apologize to one another. When they are caught having wronged someone, they confess—but they never say they're sorry. It's as if the factual statement of guilt matters more than having any feeling about it. Sorrow goes out with the other 93 percent.

As if desensitized by all this disembodiment, young people also exhibit an almost compensatory exhibitionism. Kids on social networking sites and video channels share explicit photos of themselves, not just for money or items on their "wish lists" but simply to get noticed. They seem not to know—or to care—that everything they post remains permanent, ready to haunt them as they seek jobs or spouses in the future. We might find some solace in the sensibility of the net's most techno-progressive young people, who tend to believe that the loss of privacy and collapse of identity they're currently wrestling with online is preparation—a trial run—for a human future in which people enjoy full telepathic powers. They believe that they are getting a taste of what it is like to see inside other people's heads now in order to be able to handle the full sharing of all thought in some evolutionary future. We'll see about that. Less speculatively, all this over-sharing online is also a predictable reaction to spending so much time in a disembodied realm where nothing seems to stick, and nothing registers on a fully felt level. The easiest response is to pump up the volume and intensity.

---

5. Sherry Turkle, *Alone Together: Why We Expect More from Technology and Less from Each Other* (New York: Basic Books, 2011).

Sadly for young people, the digital realm is permanent. This robs from them the free experimentation that defines one's adolescence. While parents might not relish pondering what happens between teens in the back seats of their cars or behind the bleachers on a Friday night, this experimentation isn't being recorded in a database likely to outlast whatever was chiseled onto the walls of the Parthenon.

And this permanence, once fully realized and experienced, only pushes the more cynical user to increasing layers of anonymity. After all, if every comment we make to blogs or articles might be used by a future employer to evaluate our suitability for a job, we might as well say nothing—at least not with our name attached.

But caving in to this sentiment has real costs: the civility of the net, the integrity of our self-expression, and—perhaps most significantly—the openness of our society. Once we surrender to the status of the anonymous, our resentment at having to do so will seep into our posts. We become even less present than we are to begin with, less responsible for what we do, and less likely to sense the impact we are having on others. We become yet more anonymous actors in a culture where it's hard enough not to antagonize the people we know—much less those with whom we interact namelessly and facelessly.

On the other hand, maintaining a strict sense of identity online is liberating, even empowering. We realize that nothing we commit to the net is truly off the record, and learn not to say anything we aren't proud to see quoted, shared, and linked to.

We don't put words into the digital realm unless we are willing to own them.

VII. SOCIAL

Do Not Sell Your Friends

In spite of its many dehumanizing tendencies, digital media is still biased toward the social. In the ongoing coevolution between people and technologies, tools that connect us thrive—and tools that don't connect us soon learn to. We must remember that the bias of digital media is toward contact with other people, not with their content or, worse, their cash. If we don't, we risk robbing ourselves of the main gift digital technology has to offer us in return for our having created it.

Almost immediately after the first computer networks were developed for Defense Department use, their system operators noticed something strange: the scientists who had accounts were spending more time and bandwidth talking about their personal research interests and favorite science fiction novels than official business.

While the Internet—then Arpanet—was a technological success, it had become overwhelmed by social use. The government decided to give it away. AT&T turned down the offer to take it over. In what may have ultimately been a kind of wisdom, they couldn't see a business application for what appeared to be an academic social scene. The government ended up setting the net free, to a large extent, with the proviso that it only be used for research purposes.

No one thought the net would end up going anywhere—not least of which because people conversing with one another over networks seemed to be a financial dead end. The net was compared to Citizens Band radio—a two-year fad that faded even before a movie about the truck drivers' lingo and culture could be shot and released. My own first Internet book was actually canceled by the publisher in 1992 because they thought the net would be "over" by 1993, when the book would finally hit the shelves.

The social, noncommercial net continued to grow and grow. By 1994, studies showed that families owning a computer modem were watching an average of nine hours less television per week. Worse, at least to marketers, they were spending it in a completely commercial-free medium. Finally, after a series of violations by small businesses looking to promote their services online, the net was opened for commercial use. Legislators used the argument that it couldn't be held back effectively anyway.

At last, businesses were free to use the net to peddle their wares. Everyone got involved, putting a "dot-com" behind every word imaginable. And while a few businesses actually succeeded online, most of them failed—miserably enough to take the stock market down with them.

This wasn't entirely the net's fault. The stock market had been looking for a new, exciting sector to lead it upward ever since the biotech crash of the 1980s. Digital media, suddenly unleashed to become the electronic strip mall for the twenty-first century, seemed like a great new place for all that investment money to flow. Problem is, most Internet businesses didn't really need all that venture capital—much less common stock. Three hackers in a garage were capable of building most online businesses for a couple of thousand dollars in pizza. Besides, Internet users were spending more time in chat rooms and conferences than on the intentionally "sticky" and heavy-handed sales sites of stores. And they were constitutionally and habitually opposed to paying for anything on a medium that had always been free.

We didn't want stuff, anyway; we wanted one another. The dot-com boom was followed by an even louder dot-com crash. And most people—at least most businesspeople and journalists—seemed to the think the net was over.

Left to our own devices, however, net users began to blog. And link. And comment. The manic investment of the dot-com boom had given us a robust network and fast connections, with which we could now do as we pleased. The web still had businesses on it, but the vast majority of connections and conversations were between people. It turned out, content is not king—*contact* is. And so what we now call "social media" was born.

Smarter businesses took notice. AOL, GeoCities, Friendster, Orkut, MySpace, and Facebook have each risen to channel all this social energy into a single, centralized location where it can be monetized. Successive rounds of investors figure that in all these digital connections and exchanges there must some marketing research to sell, some modeling that can be done, or some way to turn people's contacts into sales leads.

What all these social networking businesses keep getting wrong, however, is that the net is not *becoming* a social medium. It already *is* one. The history of the Internet can probably best be understood as a social medium repeatedly shaking off attempts to turn it into something else. And it will keep doing so. **Our digital networks are biased toward social connections—toward *contact*. Any effort to redefine or hijack those connections for profit end up compromising the integrity of the network itself, and compromising the real promise of contact.**

People are able to sense when a social network is really serving some other purpose. Seemingly permanent monopolies on our online social activity lose their constituencies more quickly than they earn them. When one network begins to sink, users flock to the next one, rebuild their contact networks, and then go on with their socializing. Yes, each commercial social networking site—no matter how seemingly permanent—will ultimately go the way of its predecessors. This is why I have attempted to use so few brand names in this book. The leading players seem permanent to us in the moment, but are forgotten just as quickly as they once took over the headlines. Remember Compuserve? Or America Online? How about MySpace? The social bias of the medium rejects the business bias of any particular venue.

This essential bias is consistently misunderstood and mischaracterized as fear or selfishness on the part of net users. The anger people feel over a social networking site's ever-changing policies really has less to do with any invasion of their privacy than the monetization of their friendships. The information gleaned from their activity is being used for other than social purposes—and this feels creepy. Friends are not bought and sold.

Yet this is precisely what most Internet businesses are trying to do. Every company of every size is looking for a "social strategy" through which to extend its brand. Each company wants to build its own social network of customers—or to build pages in existing social networks and win "friends," "fans," or "likes" from the millions of potential users out there. It's as if having what amounts to an email list will breathe life into brands already decimated by the Internet's powers of deconstruction and transparency.

What they don't yet realize, however, is that it is too late for a business to go social. Every business already is social. Transparency is no longer a choice for businesses in the Internet age—it is a given. Where there are people, there will be conversations. Those conversations are already happening, with or without any particular company's page or hub. The truth about what they do and how well they do it is already a topic of conversation.

The real way to "go social," if they wanted to, would not be to accumulate more page friends or message followers, but rather to get their friends and followers to befriend and follow one another. That's how to create a culture in a peer-to-peer, networked medium. Instead of looking to monetize or otherwise intercede between existing social connections, those promoting networks should be looking to foster connections between people who are as yet unknown to each other yet potentially in need of each other. And then let them go about their business—or their socializing.

The danger, of course, is that today's "penny for your friends" social networks will survive long enough—at least one after the other—for their compromised social standards to become accepted or even internalized by users. Kids growing up as members of networks devised to exploit their social lives are not nearly as scandalized by all this as those of us who still hold on to the ideal of genuine, agenda-free connections between people. If the social urge online comes to be understood as something necessarily comingled with commercial exploitation, then this will become the new normative human behavior as well.

Many people—and not just young people—are already incapable of seeing any ethical drawback to misrepresenting themselves to their online friends. "So what if I'm getting paid to tell everyone in my network that I'm a fan of a band I've never heard of before?" "Everyone is doing it." "Caveat emptor—let the buyer beware." The problem is, these people are not talking to buyers, but to friends. They don't even experience their online social networks as somehow separate from their personal lives, but one and the same. Unlike the businessman who is ruthless on the job and loving at home, they are equally ruthless with friends and strangers alike. This may be more consistent, but it is hardly more evolved. It's equal opportunity exploitation.

Who ends up exploited most, of course, is the person who has been convinced to behave this way. And that's where some awareness of how particular interfaces, tools, and programs influence our behavior is so valuable.

Social networking sites are filled with features, games, and activities that are compellingly addictive yet ultimately more rewarding to the network's owners than its members. Taking an action in a game instantly (and usually invisibly) turns one's entire network into a spam distribution list—selling her friends, and her friends-of-friends, to the game's real clients: market researchers and advertisers. Instead of being rewarded with cash, the player is rewarded with game points, new abilities, or in-world treasures for each further infringement on her social network. Does it feel like bribery? Not really. It's just the rules of the game. Once the first few social barriers have been broken down, the stakes inside the game world begin to feel more real than the risk of insulting some "friend" in the social networking site, anyway. Those aren't real friends, anyway. They are just fodder for the game.

Sadly, though, they *were* real friends. Whether forged online or in the real world, these virtual connections are an extension of our social reality. These are the people who help us find the right doctor when we are sick, who support us when we're out of work, and who comfort us when we lose a relative. They're the ones who help us find a couch to sleep on when we're traveling, a decent party to go to on Saturday night, or the right graduate program for a cross-disciplinary research interest. Finally though, all these contacts are less valuable for the particular things they might do for us than for the mere fact that they are they are connected to us at all.

Friendships, both digital and incarnate, do create value. But this doesn't mean the people in our lives can be understood as commodities to be collected and counted. People are not things to be sold piecemeal, but living members of a network whose value can only be realized in a free-flowing and social context. We have yet to find out what that value might be.

Content was never king, contact is. Yet the possibilities for new levels of human connectedness and collaboration offered by networking technologies have hardly been tapped. We are too slow to realize that people are not a form of content—a resource to be bought and sold; they are fellow cells in the greater organism of which we are all a part but are barely aware. We value our increased contacts for what they might provide and miss the greater value of the contact itself.

But it is this contact, this desire to construct a social organism together, that has been the driving force of digital technology all along. The instinct for increased contact is the evolutionary imperative we feel to become something greater than ourselves. Just as atoms combined into molecules, molecules clustered into cells, and cells collected into organisms, we organisms are networking into greater levels of organization.

This is the real draw of the many interactive devices we have brought into our lives. In a sense, the people dismissing the net as another form of CB radio had it right: We are still just finding novel ways of talking to one another. From the ridiculous faxes people used to send to each other containing lists of bad jokes to the tweets we now transmit by cell phone, each new communications technology provides a new excuse to forge connections.

The content is not the message, the contact is. The ping itself. It's the synaptic transmission of an organism trying to wake itself up.

VIII. FACT
Tell the Truth

The network is like a truth serum: Put something false online and it will eventually be revealed as a lie. Digital technology is biased against fiction and toward facts, against story and toward reality. This means the only option for those communicating in these spaces is to tell the truth.

Before what we think of as media even existed, the majority of our information exchange took place at the bazaar—the market and social space where people gathered to buy and sell goods, meet up with friends and, probably most importantly, learn what was happening in their world. While people may have actually spoken more at home, they were only exposed to new ideas when they entered the social and commercial realm of the bazaar. Everything took place there, from romance to betting to entertainment to shopping. Even the Torah was read on market days, for these were the only times a crowd would show up in one place.

    The activity of the bazaar was characterized by a multiplicity of interests and connections, all overlapping. Religion mixed with politics, romance mixed with commerce, and entertainment mixed with money-lending. Everyone was speaking with everybody else, and about all sorts of things and ideas. The bread man might share news of a friend's wedding engagement, while the priest might have a recommendation of a new blacksmith. And while there were certainly a few storytellers—usually foreigners bringing the tales of other cultures—the majority of the interactions between people were based in nonfiction. They talked about their products (who was selling the best fruit that day), gossip (who was sleeping with whom), weather, crops, local news, or even church politics. People exchanged the ideas, rumors, and facts that mattered to them. The only mythological material came to them from the scroll read to them by a rabbi, or as ritual recited by a priest. The interactive medium of the day—conversation—was almost entirely based in facts.

All of this information exchange allowed people to improve on themselves and their situations. The ideas passing between them—what we now call "memes" (rhymes with teams)—behaved like genes. Memes passed from person to person, and replicated if they were useful and powerful or died out if they were not. Just as a species can get stronger through natural selection of genes, a society gets stronger through the natural selection of memes. Memes are just ideas that spread. The meme for exchanging grain receipts works better than the one for depending entirely on one-to-one bartering, and so the meme spreads and many towns develop coinage. Someone else has an idea for a second gear in the windmill mechanism. It works well, and so as other millers learn of the innovation, the meme for a second gear replicates and spreads. So does the meme for "Joe makes better shoes than Sam," or "plant the seeds a week later this year." We spread the ideas that we think are true, because this will increase our value to others.

This is how the bazaar turned a feudal society of peasants into a new thriving middle class. It was a culture, constantly churning, mixing, and improving as individuals sought to improve their status. By the Late Middle Ages, the bazaar was working so well as a peer-to-peer economy that the aristocracy began to fall. As the former peasants rose to become a middle class of merchants and craftspeople, they were no longer dependent on feudal lords for food and protection. Families who had been in power for centuries were losing ground.

The royals hired some finance experts to help them reverse the trend, and they came up with two major innovations. The first, centralized currency, required that no one use any means of exchange other than the coin of the realm—which had to be borrowed from the royal treasury, at interest. This was an easy way for people who already had money (the aristocracy) to make money simply by *having* money. The second invention, the chartered corporation, prohibited anyone from competing against one of the king's officially sanctioned monopolies. Simply stated, no one could be in business for himself anymore, but had to work for one of the companies in which the king had invested.

So the peer-to-peer bazaar that almost brought down feudalism was dismantled, and feudalism evolved into what we now think of as corporate capitalism. Sadly, along with the peer-to-peer economy went peer-to-peer communication. Companies tried to replace what had been relationships between people with relationships to brands. Instead of buying your beer from Bob the brewer, you'd buy it from the officially sanctioned monopoly. The seal on the bottle was to substitute for whatever human relationship existed before. To make this transition work, brands turned to the sorts of mythologies still in use today. The Quaker on a package of oats has nothing to do with the grain in the box; he is a story.

As the Industrial Age gathered steam, more products— even more disconnected from their producers—needed to be sold. Ad agencies developed powerful brands to camouflage the factory-based origins of most of what people consumed. Industrial agriculture became the valley of a green giant, and factory-made cookies became the work of little elves working in a hollow tree. Mass media arose to disseminate all of these new myths, utterly devoid of facts. And as long as media remained a top-down proposition, there was very little fact-based, peer-to-peer communication to challenge any of it. People were working hard on assembly lines or in cubicles anyway, no longer experiencing themselves in their multiple social roles simultaneously. They were workers on the job trying to earn a paycheck, and consumers at home relaxing to the mythological drone of mass media.

Digital technology broke this.

The fundamental difference between mass media and digital media is interactivity. Books, radio, and television are "read only" media. We watch, but only have a choice over how we will react to the media someone else has made. This is why they are so good for storytelling: We are in the story-teller's world and can't talk back. Digital media, on the other hand, are "read-write." Any digital file that is playable is also sharable and changeable. (Files can be locked, at least until hackers figure out how to break the lock, but such protection is ultimately against the bias of the medium. That's why it so rarely works.) As a result, we are transitioning from a mass media that makes its stories sacred, to an interactive media that makes communication mutable and alive.

Likewise, and in stark opposition to the media monopolies of broadcast radio and television, digital communications technologies are based on networks and sharing. The original reason computers were networked to one another was so that they could share processing resources. This makes them biased toward peer-to-peer activity. Mass media respected only the law of gravity: The people with the presses or broadcast facilities dropped their myths down onto the masses. Digital media go up, down, and sideways. In a sense there is no longer any up or down at all, as each node in the network can receive the message or refuse it, change it or leave it alone, and delete it or pass it on.

We're back in the bazaar. Only instead of individuals conversing one-on-one with our local friends and associates, each of us has a global reach greater than that of most broadcast television networks. Any one of our blog posts or tweets can end up becoming the next runaway meme, reaching millions of fellow users in hours—each of whom is free to comment, remix, and mutate the original. And once again, we are no longer confined to our arbitrarily limited and distinct roles of workers or consumers. We are at once consumers, producers, investors, critics, and more, capable of breaking down the myths of mainstream media and revealing truths to one another. People are connected to one another on more than one basis again.

It's hard for any company to maintain its mythology (much less its monopoly) in such an environment. As we transform from media consumers back to cultural communicators, we message one another seeking approval and reinforcement. Myths and narratives will always be deconstructed, and mistruths eventually corrected. **The bias of our interactions in digital media shifts back toward the nonfiction on which we all depend to make sense of our world, get the most done, and have the most fun. The more valuable, truthful, and real our messages, the more they will spread and better we will do. We must learn to tell the truth.**

Sometimes it's the most negative truths that spread the best and fastest: a sports hero in a sex scandal, a celebrity porn tape, a terrible crime, or an urban legend that goes "viral." Yet even in the worst of those cases, the rumor is usually based either on an underlying truth or a cultural issue that has not been adequately addressed by its target. That's why people are compelled to repeat it when they hear it. Whether it's the news of a disowned princess dying in a car crash or a presidential candidate whose father is not a citizen, the untruths that spin out from there are just the uncontrolled mutations of people succumbing to some of the other biases of digital media. The information is still being presented and accepted as fact by newly minted digital citizens working against centuries of mythological control. They are not yet particularly adept at discerning the truth. Even though the facts they believe may be wrong, they are still committed to the nonfiction style of communication.

The same is true for traditional media, where "reality" programs now outnumber scripted shows. Instead of watching situation comedies, we watch real people placed in outrageous situations: geeks trying to woo models, women competing to marry a millionaire who is actually a poor construction worker, or dwarves doing almost anything. By aping the nonfiction bias of net entertainment, television and other traditional formats end up reflecting only the worst side of each of digital technology's other biases. The result is violent spectacle, dehumanizing humiliation, and collective cruelty. But the underlying urge is to participate and capitalize on a culture returning to fact-based exchange. It is not an exact science.

As a person's value and connections in the digital realm become dependent on the strength of their facts and ideas, we return to a more memetic, fertile, and chaotic communications space. Once a message is launched—whether by an individual or the CEO of a Fortune 500 company—it is no longer in that person's control. How it is received, how it is changed, and whether it is replicated and transmitted is up to the network. May the best meme win.

Advertising agencies believe they have all this interactivity in hand. They look at the digital communications space as a "conversation" through which the newly empowered consumer can speak her mind to the company, ask for what she wants, and then see herself reflected in the brand. Back and forth, call and response. Of course that's just the wishful thinking of mass media professionals who have no great facts to transmit, and it's wrong on both counts: It's not a two-way conversation, and the person on the other end is no longer identifying herself as a consumer.

The digital bazaar is a many-to-many conversation among people acting in one or more of their many cultural roles. It is too turbulent to be directed or dominated—but totally accessible to the memes of almost anyone, companies included. And since big companies, nations, and organizations generally produce things that affect a lot of people, the memes they release will tend to have more relevance and replicate better. Just not predictably. So when a car company decides to give its customers the online tools to make their TV commercials for a new vehicle, the most popular videos end up being anti-commercials, critical of the gas-guzzling SUVs. These scathing satires are the ones that get passed around the net, and even rebroadcast on television. It's news. The company gets a conversation—just not the one it wants. That's because on the net, mythologies fall apart and facts rise to the surface.

Many are dedicated to promoting this phenomenon. Technology sites sponsor contests to see who can reveal the inner workings of upcoming products before the manufacturers release them—much to the consternation of Silicon Valley CEOs and their marketing departments. Meanwhile, and much more significantly, sites like WikiLeaks and Memory Hole provide cover for activists with information they want to release to the public. Whether it's damning transcripts from a corporation's board meeting or the Afghan War policy documents of the Pentagon, the real facts now have a way to rise to the surface. We may hear what these institutions are saying to us, but now we also know what they actually *did* last summer . . .

The beauty—and, for many, the horror—is that actions are even more memetic than words. In a digital communications space, the people do the talking. If a company wants to promote conversation about itself, all it really needs to do is something, anything, significant. There are companies who get on the front page of the newspaper simply for releasing an upgrade to a phone. This is less about their ability to communicate than the power and importance of their actions to so many people.

In advertising terms, this means abandoning brand mythology and returning to attributes. It may sound obvious to those of us in the real world, but marketers need to learn that the easiest way to sell stuff in the digital age is to make good stuff. The fictional story that cookies were baked by elves is no longer as important as whether the cookies are healthy, have natural ingredients, are sourced appropriately, involve slave labor, or are manufactured in an environmentally friendly fashion. The facts about the cookies—particularly the facts that are socially relevant—are what will spread online, and it will happen quite naturally as employees share these facts with their friends on social networks, and consumers share these facts with potential shareholders, and so on. Ads based on brand image will only have staying power if they happen to be contradicted by some real fact about the company; then they will be valued by bloggers as terrific, visual evidence of corporate duplicity.

Likewise, people will thrive in a digital mediaspace as they learn to share the facts they've discovered and disregard the nonsense. We all have relatives who mistakenly pass on ridiculous viral emails about corporations that will give a donation of million dollars if you pass the email to others, or a kid in a hospital who needs a blood transfusion, or a threatening virus that will your data if you don't shut down you computer immediately. It's sweet that they want to share with us; it's just a shame they don't have anything real to share. Viral media fills this need for them, giving them fake facts with which to feed digital media's bias for nonfiction contact.

Those who succeed as communicators in the new bazaar will be the ones who can quickly evaluate what they're hearing, and learn to pass on only the stuff that matters. These are the people who create more signal and less noise, and become the most valued authorities in a digital media. But the real winners will once again be those who actually discover and innovate—the people who do and find things worthy of everyone else's attention. They're the ones who give us not only good excuses to send messages to one another, but also real ways for us all create more value for one another.

The way to flourish in a mediaspace biased toward nonfiction is to tell the truth. This means having a truth to tell.

IX. OPENNESS

Share, Don't Steal

Digital networks were built for the purpose of sharing comput-
ing resources by people who were themselves sharing resources,
technologies, and credit in order to create it. This is why digital
technology is biased in favor of openness and sharing. Because
we are not used to operating in a realm with these biases, how-
ever, we often exploit the openness of others or end up exploited
ourselves. By learning the difference between sharing and steal-
ing, we can promote openness without succumbing to selfishness.

No matter how private and individual we try to make our computers, our programs, and even our files, they all slowly but surely become part of the cloud. Whether we simply back up a file by sending it to the server holding our email, or go so far as to create a website archive, we all eventually make use of computing resources we don't actually own ourselves. And, eventually, someone or something else uses something of ours, too. It's the natural tug of digital technology toward what may well be its most essential characteristic: sharing.

From the CPU at the heart of a computer distributing calculations to various coprocessors, to the single mainframe at a university serving hundreds of separate terminals, computer and network architecture has always been based on sharing resources and distributing the burden. This is the way digital technology works, so it shouldn't surprise us that the technologists building computers and networks learned to work in analogous ways.

Perhaps because they witnessed how effective distributed processing was for computers, the builders of the networks we use today based both their designs as well as their own working ethos on the principles of sharing and openness. Nodes on the Internet, for example, must be open to everyone's traffic for the network to function. Each node keeps the packets that are addressed to it and passes on the others—allowing them to continue their journey toward their destination. Servers are constantly pinging one another, asking questions, getting directions, and receiving the help they need. This is what makes the Internet so powerful, and also part of what makes the Internet so vulnerable to attack: Pretty much everything has been designed to talk to strangers and offer assistance.

This encouraged network developers to work in the same fashion. The net was built in a "gift economy" based more on sharing than profit. Everyone wanted a working network, everyone was fascinated by the development of new software tools, so everyone just did what they could to build it. This work was still funded, if indirectly. Most of the programmers were either university professors or their students, free to work for credit or satisfaction beyond mere cash.

Pretty much everything we use on the Internet today—from email and the web to streaming media and videoconferencing—was developed by this nonprofit community, and released as what they called freeware or shareware. The thrill was building the network, seeing one's own innovations accepted and extended by the rest of the community, and having one's lab or school get the credit. The boost to one's reputation could still bring financial reward in the form of job advancement or speaking fees, but the real motivator was fun and pride.

As the net became privatized and commercialized, its bias for openness and sharing remained. Only now it is often people and institutions exploiting this bias in order to steal or extract value from one another's work. **Digital technology's architecture of shared resources, as well as the gift economy through which the net was developed, have engendered a bias toward openness. It's as if our digital activity wants to be shared with others. As a culture and economy inexperienced in this sort of collaboration, however, we have great trouble distinguishing between sharing and stealing.**

In many ways—most ways, perhaps—the net's spirit of openness has successfully challenged a society too ready to lock down knowledge. Teachers, for example, used to base their authority on their exclusive access to the information their pupils wished to learn. Now that students can find out almost anything they need to online, the role of the teacher must change to that of a guide or coach—more of a partner in learning who helps the students evaluate and synthesize the data they find. Similarly, doctors and other professionals are encountering a more educated clientele. Sure, sometimes the questions people ask are silly ones, based on misleading ads from drug companies or credit agencies. Other times, however, clients demonstrate they are capable of making decisions *with* their professionals rather than surrendering their authority to them—often leading to better choices and better results.

The net's bias toward collaboration has also yielded some terrific mass participatory projects, from technologies such as the Firefox browser and Linux operating system to resources like Wikipedia. As examples of collective activity, they demonstrate our ability to work together and share the burden in order to share yet again in the tool we have gained. For many, it is a political act and a personal triumph to participate in these noncommercial projects and to do so for reasons other than money.

These experiences and tools have, in turn, engendered an online aesthetic that is itself based in sharing and repurposing the output of others. As early as the 1920s, artists called the Dadaists began cutting up text and putting it together in new ways. In the 1960s, writers and artists such as William Burroughs and Brion Gysin were experimenting with the technique, physically cutting up a newspaper or other text object into many pieces and then recombining them into new forms. They saw it as a way to break through the hypnosis of traditional media and see beyond its false imagery to the real messages and commands its controllers were trying to transmit to us without our knowledge. Digital technology has turned this technique from a fringe art form to a dominant aesthetic.

From the record "scratching" of a deejay to the cut-and-paste functions of the text editor, our media is now characterized by co-opting, repurposing, remixing, and mashing-up. It's not simply that a comic book becomes a movie that becomes a TV series, a game, and then a musical on which new comic books are based. Although slowly mutating, that's still a single story or brand moving through different possible incarnations. What we're in the midst of now is a mediaspace where every creation is fodder for every other one.

Kids repurpose the rendering engines in their video games to make movies, called "machinima," starring the characters in the game. Movies and TV shows are re-edited by fans to tell new stories and then distributed on free servers. This work is fun, creative, and even inspiring. But sometimes it also seems to cross lines. Books are quoted at length or in decontextualized pieces only to be included as part of someone else's work, and entire songs are repurposed to become the backing tracks of new ones. And almost none of the original creators—if that term still means anything—are credited for their work.

In the best light, this activity breaks through sacrosanct boundaries, challenging monopolies on culture held by institutions from the church to Walt Disney. After all, if it's out there, it's everyone's. But what, if anything, is refused to the churn? Does committing a piece of work to the digital format mean turning it over to the hive mind to do with as it pleases? What does this mean for the work we have created? Do we have any authority over it, or the context in which it is used? We applaud the teenager who mashes up a cigarette commercial to expose the duplicity of a tobacco company. But what about when a racist organization mashes up some video of your last speech to make a false point about white supremacy?

This is the liability of "processing" together. We are living in an age when thinking itself is no longer a personal activity but a collective one. We are immersed in media and swimming in the ideas of other people all the time. We do not come up with our thoughts by ourselves anymore, so it's awfully hard to keep them to ourselves once we share them. Many young people I've encountered see this rather terrifying loss of privacy and agency over our data as part of a learning curve. They see the human species evolving toward a more collective awareness, and the net's openness as a trial run for a biological reality where we all know each other's thoughts through telepathy.

Whether or not we are heading for shared consciousness, this "learning curve" should still be in effect. In short, we need to develop the manners and ethics that make living and working together under these conditions pleasant and productive for everyone.

In the digital realm, with just a bit of effort, we can see, take, and replicate anything that anybody does. There is no such thing as unbreakable copy protection. If a CD or DVD can be played, it can be copied in one way or another (even if it means losing one "generation" of digital fidelity). But the fact that we *can* copy and distribute anything that anybody does, does not make it right. Most of us could pretty easily break into a neighbor's house by shattering a single pane of glass and take what we want with little risk of getting caught. Or we could just look at their personal papers, review their tax filings and bank statements, and maybe check to see what form of birth control they use.

What stops us is not law enforcement, but the social contract. On some level, through parental training or simple logic, we understand that a world where people broke into one another's homes wouldn't be a nice place to live. We respect the concepts of ownership and privacy because we want others to do the same. Restraint is just part of being members of a civilized society.

These same social norms do not yet apply to the net, where sharing, borrowing, stealing, and repurposing are all rather mashed up themselves. That's why we tend to apply the otherwise refreshing ethos of openness so universally and, ultimately, inappropriately. Having lived under a tightly controlled mediaspace for so long, its no wonder we experience our digital freedoms this way. The music and film industries have made few friends with their draconian "digital rights management" (DRM) tools and enforcement policies. When we purchase and download certain music and movie files, we also end up installing a program from the publisher that monitors how we use the file—mainly to make sure we don't give it to anyone else. But none of us wants to have spyware on our computers, even if it's only to police the illegal sharing of files. It feels like an invasion. Besides, if we have bought a piece of music, shouldn't we be allowed to share it with our friends and family? Or even just copy it to our many listening devices?

In a sense, these DRM strategies constitute a kind of robbery themselves. In order to work, these secretly planted programs must actually utilize some of the capacity of our computer's processors. They steal cycles and memory from our machines, carrying out tasks on behalf of companies without our consent. That's stealing, too.

The desperate efforts of big business to protect its copyrights and those of its writers and artists—combined with the simplifying bias of the net—only polarizes the landscape further. Breaking copyright to steal and share music or movies becomes understood as the action of a legitimate openness movement, dedicated to access and equality for everyone. Very specific ideas about collaboration, such as open source development and Creative Commons licensing, are equated with a free-for-all revolution of openness. Down with the corporations, up with the people.

Following the logic of this side of the net wars, every-thing anybody does must be posted online, for free, with comments on. Denying the free distribution of everything prevents the hive from having a crack at it, improving it, taking it apart and putting it back together. If you don't ren-der your work unto the hive mind, then you are seen to be denying society its right to work with and repurpose your creations. Just as smart phone purchasers want the right to tinker with the software on their devices, media consumers want the right to remix and re-release the content they view. Charging money for access or, worse, asking people not to give away or change your work is attacked as selfish disregard for the foundations of open networks and open society.

What this argument misses is that the very same kinds of companies are making the same money off text, music, and movies—simply by different means. Value is still being extracted from everyone who creates content that ends up freely viewable online—whether it's me writing this book or a blogger writing posts. It's simply not being passed down anymore. The search engine company still profits off the ads accompanying every search for a text. Likewise, every "free" video by an amateur requires that amateur to buy a camera, a video-capable laptop, editing software, and a broadband connection through which to upload the completed piece onto a conglomerate-owned video server, along with most of its rights.

Value is still being extracted from the work—it's just being taken from a different place in the production cycle, and not passed down to the creators themselves. Those of us who do create for a living are told the free labor will garner us exposure necessary to get paid for something else we do— like talks or television. Of course, the people hiring us to do those appearances believe they should get us for free as well, because our live performances will help publicize our books and movies. And so it goes, all the while being characterized as the new openness of a digital society, when in fact we are less open to one another than we are to exploitation from the usual suspects at the top of the traditional food chain.

Worst of all, those of us in a position to say something about any of this are labeled elitists or Luddites—as if we are the ones attempting to repress the natural evolution of culture. Rather, it's the good old spectacle working its magic through a now-decentralized mediaspace. The results— ignorance, anger, and anti-elitism—are the same.

By confronting the biases of digital media head-on, however, we can come to terms with the seeming paradox of ownership in a digital mediaspace. On the simplest level, the problem here is that the laws we developed to protect things used to deal with real stuff. Real stuff is in limited supply. Its scarcity demands protection. Digital content, because it can be copied for free, is in infinite supply. When I steal a pair of shoes from a cobbler, his investment of time and materials have been robbed as well. When I illegally copy a song from an album, I haven't cost the musician anything; at least I haven't cost him anything more than if I had never listened to the song in the first place. He loses the opportunity cost of a new customer, but I haven't actually robbed him of the thing he made. I just copied it. Besides, why should I give him scarce money for something that can be copied infinitely for free?

The answer, of course, is that I should be paying the musician for his time and energy making the music that I am enjoying. It's a cost that should be shared by all of us who listen to it, and shared equally. This notion is alien to us. Millions of people use Wikipedia on a daily basis for their work and research, a privilege gifted to them by thousands of writers and editors contributing their time for free. Traffic is huge, but so few think to pay for it that the nonprofit foundation funding Wikipedia can barely meet the costs of maintaining its servers. The openness of the net, and the ease with which we can make use of its resources for free, makes the notion of joining the paying minority look too much like the sucker's bet in a bad game-theory scenario. But that game is rigged.

The real problem is that while our digital mediaspace is biased toward a shared cost structure, our currency system is not. We are attempting to operate a twenty-first-century digital economy on a thirteenth-century, printing press–based operating system. It doesn't work. As we have already seen, the centralized currency system we still use today was developed by a waning aristocracy looking to stifle peer-to-peer economic growth and install a system of indebtedness. It is a printing press–era strategy, in which a scarce currency loaned into existence from a central source generates competition between people for the precious jobs and goods of artificial monopolies.

Meanwhile, we now have access to a decentralizing technology that permits the creation of value from the periphery as well as the exchange of value in a peer-to-peer fashion. Instead of buying from and selling to one another through highly centralized corporations, we now have the technology required to buy from and sell to one another directly. Beyond using eBay or the less corporate Etsy or Craigslist to make those connections and conduct transactions, however, we also have the means to transcend traditional currency.

Local currencies, made illegal to make way for centralized currency during the Renaissance, have already regained widespread acceptance following the banking crisis of 2008. Instead of borrowing this money from a bank, users *earn* it into existence by making goods and performing services for other people in the same community.[6] Peer-to-peer currencies are based in the abundance of production, rather than the scarcity of lending. This makes them biased, as is the net, toward transaction and exchange rather than hoarding for interest.

Now that digital technologies offer us identity confirmation, secure transactions, and distributed networks, we have the ability to operate local-style currencies on a global scale. Net-based, or "e-currencies," have already been experimented with successfully in gaming environments, and are now under development around the world for more practical applications across great distances.

This is not as far-fetched a concept as it may appear. Even former Fed chairman Alan Greenspan sees private electronic currencies as a promising solution to the fiscal

---

6. See the LETSystems home page at http://www.gmlets.u-net.com/
    for some simple explanations of how this works. Or see the currency
    chapter in my own *Life Inc: How Corporatism Conquered the World and
    How We Can Take it Back* (New York: Random House, 2009).

challenges posed by the information age.[7] Instead of buying the things other people make through centralized banks and credit card companies, peer-to-peer currencies allow for the direct transfer of value from one person on the periphery to another. Moreover, instead of being biased toward large corporations that can borrow money less expensively than small companies and individuals, e-currencies can be biased toward the people creating the actual value.

Whether or not we are witnessing a wholesale change in the way money is created and exchanged has yet to be seen. Given the breadth and depth of change in other arenas as we move from an analog to a digital society, however, an upgrade of our currency's operating system seems within reason. The one we have been using for the past seven centuries, and the banks behind it, appear to be having a hard time keeping up. Meanwhile, if people have the opportunity to directly fund the artists, writers, and other workers from whom they buy digital goods, they might feel more inclined to pay for what they use than they do when such items are supplied by impersonal corporations.

Until that time, however, we are best governed not by what we can get away with, but how we want to be treated by others. The people on the other side of the screen spent time and energy on the things we read and watch. When we insist on consuming it for free, we are pushing them toward something much closer to the broadcast

---

7. See Alan Greenspan, "Fostering Financial Innovation: The Role of Government" in *The Future of Money in the Information Age* (Washington, DC: Cato Institute, 1997). Or watch any of Greenspan's later testimonies to Congress.

television model, where ads fund everything. We already know what that does for the quality of news and entertainment. Yet this is precisely the model that the ad-based hosts and search engines are pushing for. By encouraging us to devalue and deprofessionalize our work, these companies guarantee a mediaspace where only they get paid. They devalue the potential of the network itself to create value in new ways. It's just like free TV, except the writers and actors don't receive any income. Instead, they just pay for the equipment to create and for access to the servers they don't own.

We accept this model only because we don't know enough about how these systems work to make decisions about them intelligently. Creative Commons[8]—an alternative to copyright developed by Stanford Law professor Larry Lessig—is not a free-for-all but a social contract through which content creators can declare under what conditions someone else may use and repurpose their work: in whole, in parts, or not at all. It amounts to a statement made by an author and attached to her work. While one of these statements may ultimately be legally enforceable, it is a system depending not on the courts but on the culture. To function, the community must agree to abide by its standards.

Likewise, open source is not an invitation to take whatever you want, whenever you want it, no matter who created it or how much it cost to produce. It is a working relationship among programmers to develop software together and even capture some of the value they create. Instead of maintaining

---

8. See CreativeCommons.org for more detailed descriptions of these choices for publication without traditional copyright.

a competitive advantage by keeping their code closed and encrypted, developers keep their code open and visible for others to improve upon it. Instead of working in competing silos, programmers build off one another's innovations. Participation is dependent on knowing both the programming code necessary to make valuable additions and the social codes necessary to do it in ways that respect the contributions of others.

Digital society may always be biased toward sharing, but a real understanding of the codes through which it has been built makes stealing a nonstarter.

X. PURPOSE

Program or Be Programmed

Digital technology is programmed. This makes it biased toward those with the capacity to write the code. In a digital age, we must learn how to make the software, or risk becoming the software. It is not too difficult or too late to learn the code behind the things we use—or at least to understand that there is code behind their interfaces. Otherwise, we are at the mercy of those who do the programming, the people paying them, or even the technology itself.

One of the US Air Force generals charged with building and protecting the Global Information Grid has a problem: recruitment. As the man in charge of many of the Air Force's coolest computer toys, he has no problem attracting kids who want to fly drones, shoot lasers from satellites, or steer missiles into Persian Gulf terrorist camps from the safety of Shreveport. They're lining up for those assignments. No, the general's challenge is finding kids capable of *programming* these weapons systems—or even having the education, inclination, and mental discipline required to begin learning programming from scratch.

Raised on commercial video games that were themselves originally based on combat simulation technologies, these recruits have enviable reflexes and hand-eye coordination. They are terrific virtual pilots. Problem is, without an influx of new programmers capable of maintaining the code and fixing bugs—much less upgrading and innovating new technologies—the general cannot keep his operation at mission readiness. His last resort has been to give lectures at education conferences in which he pleads with high schools to put programming into their curriculums.

That's right: America, the country that once put men on the moon, is now falling behind most developed and many developing nations in computer education. We do not teach programming in most public schools. Instead of teaching programming, most schools with computer literacy curriculums teach *programs*. Kids learn how to use popular spreadsheet, word-processing, and browsing software so that they can operate effectively in the high-tech workplace. These basic skills may make them more employable for the entry-level cubicle jobs of today, but they will not help them adapt to the technologies of tomorrow.

Their bigger problem is that their entire orientation to computing will be from the perspective of users. When a kid is taught a piece of software as a subject, she'll tend to think of it like any other thing she has to learn. Success means learning how to behave in the way the program needs her to. Digital technology becomes the immutable thing, while the student is the movable part, conforming to the needs of the program in order to get a good grade on the test.

Meanwhile, kids in other countries—from China to Iran—aren't wasting their time learning how to use off-the-shelf commercial software packages. They are finding out how computers work. They learn computer languages, they write software and, yes, some of them are even taught the cryptography and other skills they need to breach Western cyber-security measures. According to the Air Force general, it's just a matter of a generation before they've surpassed us.

While military superiority may not be everyone's foremost goal, it can serve as a good indicator of our general competitiveness culturally and economically with the rest of the world. As we lose the ability to program the world's computers, we lose the world's computing business as well. This may not be a big deal to high-tech conglomerates who can as easily source their programming from New Delhi as New Hampshire. But it should be a big deal to us.

Instead, we see actual coding as some boring chore, a working-class skill like bricklaying, which may as well be outsourced to some poor nation while our kids play and even design video games. We look at developing the plots and characters for a game as the interesting part, and the programming as the rote task better offloaded to people somewhere else. We lose sight of the fact that the programming—the code itself—is the place from which the most significant innovations emerge.

Okay, you say, so why don't we just make sure there are a few students interested in this highly specialized area of coding so that we can keep up militarily and economically with everyone else? Just because a few of us need to know how to program, surely that doesn't mean we *all* need to know programming, does it? We all know how to drive our cars, yet few of us know how our automobiles actually work, right?

True enough, but look where that's gotten us: We spend an hour or two of what used to be free time operating a dangerous two-ton machine and, on average, a full workday each week paying to own and maintain it.[9] Throughout the twentieth century, we remained blissfully ignorant of the real biases of automotive transportation. We approached our cars as consumers, through ads, rather than as engineers or, better, civic planners. We gladly surrendered our public streetcars to private automobiles, unaware of the real expenses involved. We surrendered our highway policy to a former General Motors chief, who became secretary of defense primarily for the purpose of making public roads suitable for private cars and spending public money on a highway system. We surrendered city and town life for the commuting suburbs, unaware that the bias of the automobile was to separate home from work. As a result, we couldn't see that our national landscape was being altered to manufacture dependence on the automobile. We also missed the possibility that these vehicles could make the earth's atmosphere unfit for human life, or that we would one day be fighting wars primarily to maintain the flow of oil required to keep them running.

So considering the biases of a technology before and during its implementation may not be so trivial after all. In the case of digital technology, it is even more important than usual. The automobile determined a whole lot about how we'd get from place to place, as well as how we would reorganize our physical environment to promote its use. Digital technology doesn't merely convey our bodies, but ourselves.

---

9. The Bureau of Labor Statistics (http://www.bls.gov/) updates these figures yearly.

Our screens are the windows through which we are experiencing, organizing, and interpreting the world in which we live. They are also the interfaces through which we express who we are and what we believe to everyone else. They are fast becoming the boundaries of our perceptual and conceptual apparatus; the edge between our nervous systems and everyone else's, our understanding of the world and the world itself.

If we don't know how they work, we have no way of knowing what is really out there. We cannot truly communicate, because we have no idea how the media we are using bias the messages we are sending and receiving. Our senses and our thoughts are already clouded by our own misperceptions, prejudices, and confusion. Our digital tools add yet another layer of bias on top of that. But if we don't know what their intended and accidental biases are, we don't stand a chance of becoming coherent participants in the digital age. **Programming is the sweet spot, the high leverage point in a digital society. If we don't learn to program, we risk being programmed ourselves**.

The irony here is that computers are frightfully easy to learn. Programming is immensely powerful, but it is really no big deal to learn. Back in the 1970s, when computers were supposedly harder to use, there was no difference between operating a computer and programming one. Better public schools offered computer classes starting in the sixth or seventh grade, usually as an elective in the math department. Those of us lucky to grow up during that short window of opportunity learned to think of computers as "anything machines." They were blank slates, into which we wrote our own software. The applications we wrote were crude and often rather point-less—like teaching the computer to list prime numbers, draw pictures with text, or, as in my own final project, decide how to prioritize the decisions of an elevator car.

I'm sure only one or two of us actually graduated to become professional programmers, but that wasn't the point. All of us came to understand what programming is, how programmers make decisions, and how those decisions influence the ways the software and its users function. For us, as the mystery of computers became the science of programming, many other mysteries seemed to vanish as well. For the person who understands code, the whole world reveals itself as a series of decisions made by planners and designers for how the rest of us should live. Not just computers, but everything from the way streets are organized in a town to the way election rules (are tilted for a purpose vote for any three candidates) begin to look like what they are: sets of rules developed to promote certain outcomes. Once the biases become apparent, anything becomes possible. The world and its many arbitrary systems can be hacked.

Early computers were built by hackers, whose own biases ended up being embedded in their technologies. Computers naturally encouraged a hacker's approach to media and technology. They made people less interested in buying media and a bit more interested in making and breaking it. They also turned people's attention away from sponsored shows and toward communicating and sharing with one another. The problem was that all this communicating and sharing was bad for business.

So the people investing in software and hardware development sought to discourage this hacker's bias by making interfaces more complex. The idea was to turn the highly transparent medium of computing into a more opaque one, like television. Interfaces got thicker and more supposedly "user friendly" while the real workings of the machine got buried further in the background. The easy command-line interface (where you just type a word telling the machine what you want it to do) was replaced with clicking and dragging and pointing and watching. It's no coincidence that installing a program in Windows required us to summon "The Wizard"—not the helper, the puppy, or even that "Paper Clip Man." No, we needed the Wizard to re-mystify the simple task of dragging an application into the applications folder, and maybe a database file somewhere else. If we had been privy to everything the Wizard was doing on our behalf, then we may have even been able to uninstall the entire program without purchasing one of those hard drive sweeping utilities. Instead, we were told not to look behind the curtain.

It was all supposedly safer that way. Accepting the computer salesman's pitch as technological truth, we bought the false premise that the more open a device was to us, the more open it was to every bad person out there. Better to buy a locked-down and locked-up device, and then just trust the company we bought it from to take care of us. Like it used to say on the back of the TV set: *Hazard of electric shock. No user serviceable parts inside.* Computing and programming were to be entrusted to professionals. Consumers can decorate their desktops the way they like, and pick which programs to purchase, but heaven forbid they trust an unauthorized vendor or, worse, try to do something themselves. They must do everything through the centralized applications program, through the exclusive carrier, and not try to alter any of it. The accepted logic is that these closed technologies and systems are safer and more dependable.

Of course none of this is really true. And the only way you'd really know this is if you understood programming. Fully open and customizable operating systems, like Linux, are much more secure than closed ones such as Microsoft Windows. In fact, the back doors that commercial operating systems leave for potential vendors and consumer research have made them more vulnerable to attack than their open source counterparts. This threat is compounded by the way commercial vendors keep their source code a secret. We aren't even to know the ways we are vulnerable. We are but to trust. Even the Pentagon is discouraged from developing its own security protocols through the Linux platform, by a Congress heavily lobbied to promote Windows.[10]

Like the military, we are to think of our technologies in terms of the applications they offer right out of the box instead of how we might change them or write our own. We learn what our computers already do instead of what we can make them do. This isn't even the way a kid naturally approaches a video game. Sure, a child may play the video game as it's supposed to be played for a few dozen or hundred hours. When he gets stuck, what does he do? He goes online to find the "cheat codes" for the game. Now, with infinite ammunition or extra-strength armor, he can get through the entire game. Is he still playing the game? Yes,

---

10. See Richard Clarke, *Cyberwar: The Next Threat to National Security* (New York: HarperCollins, 2010).

but from outside the confines of the original rules. He's gone from player to cheater.

After that, if he really likes the game, he goes back online to find the modification kit—a simple set of tools that lets a more advanced user change the way the game looks and feels. So instead of running around in a dungeon fighting monsters, a kid might make a version of the game where players run around in a high school fighting their teachers—much to the chagrin of parents and educators everywhere. He uploads his version of the game to the Internet, and watches with pride as dozens or even hundreds of other kids download and play his game, and then comment about it on gamers' bulletin boards. The more open it is to modification, the more consistent software becomes with the social bias of digital media.

Finally, if the version of the game that kid has developed is popular and interesting enough, he just may get a call from a gaming company looking for new programmers. Then, instead of just creating his own components for some other programmer's game engine, he will be ready to build his own.

These stages of development—from player to cheater to modder to programmer—mirror our own developing relationship to media through the ages. In preliterate civilizations, people attempted to live their lives and appease their gods with no real sense of the rules. They just did what they could, sacrificing animals and even children along the way to appease the gods they didn't understand. The invention of text gave them a set of rules to follow—or not. Now, everyone was a cheater to some extent, at least in that they had the choice of whether to go by the law, or to evade it. With the printing press came writing. The Bible was no longer set in stone, but something to be changed—or at least reinterpreted. Martin Luther posted his ninety-five theses, the first great "mod" of Catholicism, and later, nations rewrote their histories by launching their revolutions.

Finally, the invention of digital technology gives us the ability to program: to create self-sustaining information systems, or virtual life. These are technologies that carry on long after we've created them, making future decisions without us. The digital age includes robotics, genetics, nanotechnology, and computer programs—each capable of self-regulation, self-improvement, and self-perpetuation. They can alter themselves, create new versions of themselves, and even collaborate with others. They grow. These are not just things you make and use. These are emergent forms that are biased toward their own survival. Programming in a digital age means determining the codes and rules through which our many technologies will build the future—or at least how they will start out.

The problem, as I explained in the introduction, is that we haven't actually seized the capability of each great media age. We have remained one dimensional leap behind the technology on offer. Before text, only the Pharaoh could hear the words of the gods. After text, the people could gather in the town square and hear the word of God read to them by a rabbi. But only the rabbi could read the scroll. The people remained one stage behind their elite. After the printing press a great many people learned to read, but only an elite with access to the presses had the ability to write. People didn't become authors; they became the gaming equivalent of the "cheaters" who could now read the Bible for themselves and choose which laws to follow.

Finally, we have the tools to program. Yet we are content to seize only the capability of the last great media renaissance, that of writing. We feel proud to build a web page or finish our profile on a social networking site, as if this means we are now full-fledged participants in the cyber era. We remain unaware of the biases of the programs in which we are participating, as well as the ways they circumscribe our newfound authorship within their predetermined agendas. Yes, it is a leap forward, at least in the sense that we are now capable of some active participation, but we may as well be sending text messages to the producers of a TV talent show, telling them which of their ten contestants we think sings the best. Such are the limits of our interactivity when the ways in which we are allowed to interact have been programmed for us in advance.

Our enthusiasm for digital technology about which we have little understanding and over which we have little control leads us not toward greater agency, but toward less. We end up at the mercy of voting machines with "black box" technologies known only to their programmers, whose neutrality we must accept on faith. We become dependent on search engines and smart phones developed by companies we can only hope value our productivity over their bottom lines. We learn to socialize and make friends through interfaces and networks that may be more dedicated to finding a valid advertising model than helping us find one another.

Yet again, we have surrendered the unfolding of a new technological age to a small elite who have seized the capability on offer. But while Renaissance kings maintained their monopoly over the printing presses by force, today's elite is depending on little more than our own disinterest. We are too busy wading through our overflowing inboxes to consider how they got this way, and whether there's a better or less frantic way to stay informed and in touch. We are intimidated by the whole notion of programming, seeing it as a chore for mathematically inclined menials than a language through which we can re-create the world on our own terms.

We're not just building cars or televisions sets—devices that, if we later decide we don't like, we can choose not to use. We're tinkering with the genome, building intelligent machines, and designing nanotechnologies that will continue where we leave off. The biases of the digital age will not just be those of the people who programmed it, but of the programs, machines, and life-forms they have unleashed. In the short term, we are looking at a society increasingly dependent on machines, yet decreasingly capable of making or even using them effectively. Other societies, such as China, where programming is more valued, seem destined to surpass us—unless, of course, the other forms of cultural repression in force there offset their progress as technologists. We shall see. Until push comes to shove and geopolitics force us to program or perish, however, we will likely content ourselves with the phone apps and social networks on offer. We will be driven toward the activities that help distract us from the coming challenges—or stave them off—rather than the ones that encourage us to act upon them.

But futurism is not an exact science, particularly where technology is concerned. In most cases, the real biases of a technology are not even known until that technology has had a chance to exist and replicate for a while. Technologies created for one reason usually end up having a very different use and effect. The "missed call" feature on cell phones ended up being hacked to give us text messaging. Personal computers, once connected to phone lines, ended up becoming more useful as Internet terminals. Our technologies only submit to our own needs and biases once we hack them in one way or another. We are in partnership with our digital tools, teaching them how to survive and spread by showing them how they can serve our own intentions. We do this by accepting our roles as our programs' true users, rather than subordinating ourselves to them and becoming the used.

In the long term, if we take up this challenge, we are looking at nothing less than the conscious, collective intervention of human beings in their own evolution. It's the opportunity of a civilization's lifetime. Shouldn't more of us want to participate actively in this project?

Digital technologies are different. They are not just objects, but systems embedded with purpose. They act with intention. If we don't know how they work, we won't even know what they want. The less involved and aware we are of the way our technologies are programmed and program themselves, the more narrow our choices will become; the less we will be able to envision alternatives to the pathways described by our programs; and the more our lives and experiences will be dictated by their biases.

On the other hand, the more humans become involved in their design, the more humanely inspired these tools will end up behaving. We are developing technologies and networks that have the potential to reshape our economy, our ecology, and our society more profoundly and intentionally than ever before in our collective history. As biologists now understand, our evolution as a species was not a product of random chance, but the forward momentum of matter and life seeking greater organization and awareness. This is not a moment to relinquish our participation in that development, but to step up and bring our own sense of purpose to the table. It is the moment we have been waiting for.

For those who do learn to program see the rest of the world differently as well.

Even if we don't all go out and learn to program—something any high school student can do with a decent paperback on the subject and a couple of weeks of effort—we must at least learn and contend with the essential biases of the technologies we will be living and working with from here on.

I've endeavored to explain ten of the most significant ones here, as well as how to turn them from liabilities into opportunities. But you will surely continue to find others. I encourage you to explore them, come up with your own strategies, and then share them with others—including me.

If living in the digital age teaches us anything, it is that we are all in this together. Perhaps more so than ever.

XI. AI

Value the Human

"First they came for the cab drivers, and I said nothing because I am not a cab driver . . . "

Most people who fear artificial intelligence are simply afraid for their jobs. While earlier autonomous technologies appeared to threaten only the most rote, mechanical jobs, now we are coming to realize that anyone's employment could one day be replaced by a machine or artificial intelligence.

Is this necessarily a problem? Do we all really want jobs? Or do we simply want money, food, shelter, things that bring us joy, and perhaps a sense of meaningfully contributing to the welfare of others? Becoming a true programmer of our reality may require us to distinguish between employment and the real value of humans.

It's no true crime against humanity to replace most Uber drivers with autonomous vehicles. That's because the vast majority of Uber drivers are not doing it for the fun of it, but for the money. Most of them would rather be out playing softball or making music. If we really could substitute for our labor with machines—ones that don't pollute or create even more work for someone else to mine the rare earth metals or tag all the data—it wouldn't necessarily be a problem. So far, in spite of projections to the contrary, we are nowhere close. AI doesn't really replace labor at all. It simply moves us humans further down the hierarchy of skills. It's like the dumbwaiter, which didn't really save Thomas Jefferson's enslaved servants any labor—it just spared Jefferson and his guests the indignity of actually interacting with the enslaved human servant. They were still there, just more hidden. Likewise, an AI may take the job of a driver, a writer, or a lawyer, but it requires the work of legions of people to mine for the rare earth metals, get the cobalt out of lakes, tag all the data that it's fed, and so on. It doesn't simply take our jobs, it down-skills our labor.

But let's say things change, and AI's really become capable of doing our work without creating more labor, pollution, and suffering in the process. If this were really the case, then we would simply have to learn to feel okay about letting people live and enjoy the bounty of a high-tech society without necessarily contributing to the industrial economy. Having more than enough of everything shouldn't be a problem, and if technology really could usher in that reality we shouldn't prevent it simply because we don't yet have an *economic* program that can contend with universal prosperity.[11] This is what it means to recognize what aspects of our world are programmable, and then taking command of them.

This doesn't mean that all human functions can be replaced with machines. The human difference is that we have the capacity for true creativity. AI's are fine for industry.

---

11 See my book *Throwing Rocks at the Google Bus: How Growth Became the Enemy of Prosperity* for some ideas on how that could work.

They're a product of Industrial Age thinking, and reinforce its values. They do not create, they model. That's what "large language models" means. Just like computers "model" a typewriter as a word processor, or a complex weather system in order to predict the future, AI's model writing or composing by looking at all the texts and songs in their databases or out on the internet and then generating an approximate average. They model the most typical version of something possible.

Now that's fine for certain forms of entertainment. Maybe a Marvel movie, or, better, a roller coaster. An AI can look at all the successful roller coasters out there, measure the effects on riders, and come up with increasingly idealized combinations of drops and loops and spirals. Aristotle considered such "spectacle" the lowest form of entertainment, almost like cheating when compared with more meaningful expressions such as character development or plot. Like Las Vegas fireworks instead of a Shakespeare soliloquy. But it has its place, particularly in an entertainment industry where formula is more important than personal expression or audience insight.

Still, most AI creations—or outputs—are far less interesting as finished products than they were to the people who interacted with the AI's in order to make them. Most AI-created paintings look like airbrushed fantasy comics of the 1980s, hyperrealistic anime movies, or whatever aesthetic they're copying. AI-generated movie clips may be technically impressive, but are as forgettable as any science-fiction movie trailer.

Instead of using AI to commodify all the arts and entertainment that went before it, what about celebrating AI as its own form of entertainment? When we use AI to make a movie or a book, no one gets to see the AI at work, interact with it, or experience those weird uncanny-valley moments that make AI so interesting to its developers. We see the finished product, which is about as interesting as looking at wallpaper.

Looking at someone's Midjourney picture is like listening to them talk about their psychedelic trip. You had to be there. Likewise, the value of AI is the opportunity to play with the AI itself. No matter how cliche their results, people often claim to have had truly profound experiences iterating those projects with the AI's. That's because they have been in the position of what we must ultimately consider the programmer instead of the programmed, and participated in the process of attempting to model or even impact reality with technology. This focus on the ongoing human process of modeling over the apparent value of the models themselves has defined the programmer's sensibility since the emergence of digital technology in the 1980s. AI is now helping make this distinction clearer for everyone.

It's easy to forget how digital technology and the early Internet looked to us back then. Some folks—mainly business types—were talking about the "digital revolution," but for programmers and creatives, it was more of "renaissance." We wouldn't simply replace one elite with another. We were not, as a revolution implies, drawing a circle. Rather, we were—as re-naissance suggests—retrieving and rebirthing old ideas in a new context. Just as the original Renaissance increased our appreciation for dimensionality with perspective painting and circumnavigating the spherical world, our renaissance would increase our appreciation for dimensionality with holograms, or by orbiting the planet with satellites.

The defining image of this early digital sensibility was the fractal. Until the fractal, we used Euclidian geometry to understand our world. This meant measuring the volume of clouds as if they were spheres, or the coastlines of islands as if they were polygons. In order to contend with something as chaotic as the ocean, you just superimposed a grid of latitude and longitude lines over it. Does the ocean have anything to do with that grid? Of course not, but it's a way to describe a simple location without having to deal with all those complex wave patterns. You just ignore them. That tendency to oversimplify, and to relate things from the real world to idealized and abstracted shapes, informed everything we did, from monocultural crops to city planning to capitalism.

But with computers, we gained the ability to calculate in new ways. Benoit Mandlebrot, a mathematician at IBM, was trying to find new ways to predict the seemingly random interference on phone lines, when he came up with the idea of using non-linear equations. Instead of looking for a simple equation, like $2x + 1 = y$ and coming up with an answer, he got the idea of using the feedback loops of computers to feed each answer back into the equation. (Feedback is what you get when you point a microphone at its own speaker. It listens to its own noise, and feeds it back into the system again and again until you hear that screech.) So instead of just getting an answer of y, he'd put that answer back in the equation as the new x. (Most simply, that means if you started with $x = 1$, you'd get answer of $2x1 + 1 = 3$. Then you take 3 as the new x, and get $2x3 + 1 = 7$, and then plug in that 7, and so on and so on.)

While the graphs of those simple equations will draw a simple line or curve, he used more complicated equations and got much more complex graphs. That's what we called fractals—those paisley psychedelic patterns that looked like fern plants, coral reefs, galaxies, and other natural phenomena.

We were all thrilled. It seemed as if the oversimplified classical ideals we had been using to impose colonialism, capitalism, and all sorts of other -isms on the natural world would be overturned, in favor of these new chaos-embracing modeling systems. Instead of turning to the cartographer to tell us that a particular point in the ocean was this many degrees latitude or longitude, we'd embrace the surfer's mentality and contend directly with the complexity of the waves themselves. Armed with these nonlinear feedback loops, computers would be able to model anything.

What we didn't take into account, however, at least not immediately, was that these models were not reality. They were really just an awful lot like reality. Yes, fractals and other digitally rendered systems looked like ferns, coral reefs, galaxies, weather systems, and so on, but they were just models of these things. They were more complex than simple maps, but their apparent complexity camouflaged their artifice. They're really really cool. You can zoom in on any section and it will continue to render gorgeous, self-similar patterns. And these models can yield terrific answers, new ways of framing and seeing and understanding systems, of farming, or running societies . . . but they're still abstracted and disconnected from reality. They can build a metropolis with a complexity closer to *SimCity* than to a board game like Monopoly. But they're still just models.

And we keep forgetting this. Every time computers move up a notch, or do something seemingly more complex, we begin to think, "this time it really is going to do it." The web seemed as complex as reality until the dotcom boom reminded us it was just a series of business plans. Then Web 2.0 and social media were supposed to do it. Then ultra-fast trading, derivatives, and algorithms. Then it was the blockchain that would finally be able to record and instrumentalize every single aspect of reality.

Today, it's what tech investors are calling artificial intelligence, but what would more accurately be called Large Language Models. LLMs work by searching through everything that's ever been posted on the Internet or a database, and then assembling the most probable string of words in response to any question or statement. It is, quite literally, the average of all the writing and thinking about a particular question or idea. Yet many people think we're creating life itself. We are not. We are really just creating another layer of abstraction: a way of mining all the rhetoric we've put out there and then synthesizing it into forms that simulate language without using any knowledge or thought. Real thinking is to an AI like ocean waves are to a latitude line.

In an AI, there is genuinely no one home. It's all model. No reality. It's looking at everything we've ever modeled—or at least all the models that we've digitized (and that human beings have tagged for it) and then developing language around those models. It's all a form of auto-tuning and auto-completion—of taking what has already happened and putting it back together in the most statistically probable way. It does not create anything. It simply models things.

Still, interestingly enough, AI's facility with models may actually be of service to us humans as we strive to distinguish our models from our reality, and our simulations from life. What better than an AI to distinguish between AI-generated disinformation and real news? Unlike humans, AI's can actually access all the models out there at once. The same features that allow AI's to source material from everywhere allow them to recognize whether something else has been sourced and composed from the same slush pile of prior creations.

The truly killer app for AI's in our current civilization may be to serve as digital informants. They can observe and tattle on each other, revealing when something supposedly real is just one of their fellow AI's creations. But more importantly, they can help remind us when something is just a map, a model, or a social construction rather than a given circumstance of nature. From the money in our pockets to the fact that we need a car to get to work, or that we need to be employed at all or that we need to pay rent to some landlord in order to be allowed to sleep in an apartment. They are all programmed.

When we're born into such a world, of course we accept such conventions at face value. It's how things are. But the trick to moving beyond them is to alienate ourselves from them, and learn to recognize their artificiality and embedded agendas so that we can program them differently. As the ultimate modeling machines, AI's may just be able to help us do that. Their job is not to create even more compelling models (as they are currently being deployed) but to recognize that the money in your pocket is not value, but a particular form of currency designed to keep a particular class of people in power. AI's can trace the origins of the social programs leading us to accept extractive and self-defeating approaches to work and life, while also recognizing the synthetic behaviors of all the other bots out there trying to fool us into adopting one destructive model or another.

Maybe, just maybe, AI's can become the next and last generation of feedback loop, exposing the false promise of the totalizing systems of the digital age, whose higher levels of complexity still don't mean a thing to those of us living here on the ground, attempting to flourish together through a myriad spectrum of value exchanges we don't even know how to perceive or measure, much less model. None of that stuff is in the models because none of it has even been consciously sensed, recognized, labeled, or recorded.

Our renaissance must not be an affirmation of the last one's abstracted ideals at greater resolution or rendered with greater complexity. (Second verse, same as the first . . .) It must instead be a reclamation of the more experiential, ineffable, and irresolvable qualities of real life. We can't fight over these created models and histories anymore. They cannot be resolved. They are not real. They are models. Games. Rhetoric. Approximations. They are figures, and never ground.

Afterword to the 2024 Edition

Programming the World

Many tech developers and entrepreneurs have come to understand a lot of what I shared in this book. They are aware of the various harms and externalities of the technologies they have built and want to reverse some of these media effects. As if seeing the light, they now want to create apps and platforms that undo the problems that their original apps and platforms caused. So they create meditation apps to calm minds that have been intentionally made anxious by social media, or wellness platforms to "nudge" people toward healthier uses of their time than doomscrolling on a new app. There are even whole organizations and institutes dedicated to developing "humane technologies" that treat people more benevolently than their predecessors.

But the orientation of these efforts is all wrong. They're all about using technology on people, rather than people using technology themselves. "Humane" is the way companies claim to treat cage-free chickens: a commitment by an industry to raise and slaughter its living commodities as painlessly as possible. As this book has argued, however, that's not good enough. The question should not be about how humanely our technologies program human beings, but about how well human beings can program technology.

This same premise applies to any effort at social change: Are we trying to program people to behave better, or are we creating better conditions for such positive change to take place? If we want to change the cultural and economic climate from extractive digital industrialism to something more human centered, we don't do this by manipulating or reprogramming people. That only exacerbates the problem. It's an artifact of the dominating, colonialist mindset of the social programmer.

Whenever we hear talk of "getting people" to be more generous, more concerned about the climate, more committed to social justice, or even more compliant with health mandates, we must pause and reconsider. Improving our social capacities, encouraging our civic duty, and retrieving our human sensibilities are terrific goals, but we don't achieve them by attempting to engineer human behavior. Even the crafting and deployment of "memes" is really just a form of programming. The meme is like the software, and the brain is like the hardware. Once a person sees a meme, they are compelled to spread it. Memetic engineering amounts to a way of manipulating people—operating them as if they were robots—rather than providing them with the tools they need to navigate and influence the world.

Using tech or techniques on people is a form of Industrial Age thinking, reducing people to robots and human culture to operating systems. It's the soulless landscape of auto-tuning and the manufacturing of consent. True cultural change requires transcending this mindset. Instead of "getting people" to do one thing or another, we engender a culture or landscape where new possibilities and alternative approaches are likely to spawn and spread.

Over the course of my career, I've identified four "interventions" I'd like to propose to you here, as an afterword to what I consider my most important contribution to the discussion of our migration to the digital media environment.

1. Denaturalize Power.

This simply means helping people recognize the underlying assumptions embedded in our world: inventions and social constructions that we mistake for conditions of nature. We are mistaking the maps for the territory, and must work to reveal their origins, manufacture, biases, and agendas. We can play "spoilsport" to the accepted game and reveal it as a human construction.

For instance, while giving a recent television interview about promise and peril in AI, I was asked about the "unemployment problem." What would we do about all the jobs that would be lost to AI? I paused, then almost jokingly responded, "What if it's not an unemployment problem but the unemployment solution?" Who wants a job, really, anyway? Jobs are a rather recent invention, in fact, created after the establishment of "chartered monopolies" that made it illegal for any small business to compete with one of the king's officially chartered companies. Instead of making shoes and selling them at the market, the cobbler now had to work for His Majesty's Royal Shoe Company—a favored merchant who offered a kickback to the Crown for the exclusive right to monopolize the sector.

That was the moment in history when the clock went on the highest tower in the town, as if to "naturalize" the human invention of wage labor. Until that moment, the only people who sold their time were indentured servants. Five hundred years later, we accept such employment as a condition of nature. This is the history I chronicled in my book *Life Inc.*, which sought to demonstrate that both central currency and corporations were invented by particular people with particular agendas at a particular moment in history. We need not accept them as fixed features of our world.

Denaturalizing power means revealing such social constructions as inventions of people, not preexisting conditions of reality. Are we really here to serve the economy, or is it here to serve us? Do technology businesses really need to grow exponentially and have an "exit" in order to be successful? Why do we each need to save enough money in our working years to support ourselves in retirement? Why do cryptocurrencies have to support investors betting on the rising value of a token, rather than people who want to transact in a less expensive way? Does crypto have to reify the values of traditional central currency, or can it reveal and challenge them?

2. Trigger Agency.

The first time I used a word-processing program was in the computer lab at college. When I was ready to save my file, the graduate student supervising the lab asked me how I wanted to save my file: as a "protected" file that no one else could open, a "read-only" file that other people could open, or a "read-write" file that people could not only open but also *change*. I'll never forget how that concept stayed with me as I left the lab and considered the other media and institutions in my world. Which things were read-only, and which were read-write? And why?

Why is money read-only? Or religion? What if we could change them? How much of the world is arbitrarily protected from our intervention, who got to make those decisions, and what happens if we violate them? I had been raised in the read-only media environment of television, and learned to be a spectator. Might the read-write possibilities of the digital environment grant me greater access to the dashboard of civilization?

By denaturalizing power, we reveal that the codes we have been living by are actually written by people to favor their own interests. This then triggers our sense of agency to change them. Most of the social and economic laws we accept at face value were written in the era of the printing press, or, at best, the age of top-down broadcast media. A digital environment offers us new possibilities of access, authorship, and agency. We are free to develop, as I explained in the last chapter of this book, from player to cheater to author to programmer—and not just online, but in everything.

I'm not calling for a revolution here, but a change in orientation. The laws we accept as sacred inviolable truths are not from God at all, but fungible human artifacts we can adapt or discard. We mustn't mistake this open-source sensibility for the accelerationist anti-institutionalism of those who want to tear down the mechanisms of democracy altogether. Rather, we can reclaim the capacity to revise, rescript, and reprogram them ourselves. We can retrieve the functions that our institutions have failed to deliver and find new ways to fulfill them.

This book was expressed as "commands" rather than "commandments" because I am hoping to shift our orientation from rule followers to rule creators. We are in charge here.

3. Resocialize People.

In order to do any of this, we must learn to work together and recognize that—contrary to our current social maps—being human is a team sport. This was the message of my *Team Human* manifesto. We were taught in school that nature is an entirely competitive affair. Radical libertarians, in particular, like to point out that we are living in a Darwinian battle for survival of the fittest individual.

If we actually read Darwin, however, we find that he was not depicting a competitive world at all. Rather, on page after page he was marveling at the ways that species cooperate and collaborate among themselves and with each other to ensure mutual survival. As more recent science has revealed, trees in the forest don't compete for sunlight. The larger deciduous trees don't shade and steal light from their smaller counterparts, but share energy with them through an underground network of roots and mycelium. Then, when they lose their leaves in the winter, the smaller evergreen trees return energy back to them.

Likewise, under the assumptions of a digital media environment, Marx is understood as a top-down systems theorist looking to impose big solutions, at scale, on whole nations or continents. Socialism sounds like a totalizing operating system on the order of capitalism or globalism. But social-ism was actually meant to retrieve the pre-industrial social reality that allowed for the creation and exchange of value between real people. Not everything goes on the ledger. Many of our exchanges are purely social, even if real value like food or services is offered.

Resocializing people simply means making it easier for people to ask each other for favors, to establish rapport, and to build solidarity. Why are so many of us reluctant to borrow a tool from a neighbor instead of buying a new one from the store? Are we afraid to owe them a favor? Are we worried about the tool company having to lay off workers? Is there really no way for us to work less as we share more of what we have in abundance? Once we are socialized, "economics" becomes a last resort—not the default operating system but a fallback mechanism for when the social fabric has torn.

Being human is a team sport. The extent to which we may represent the most evolved species reflects how well we have learned to communicate and collaborate. While digital technology undermines these social mechanisms, real-world face-to-face contact recalibrates our nervous systems, and establishes the rapport required to achieve solidarity. We cannot denaturalize power or trigger agency alone.

4. Cultivate Awe.

Our experiences of collectivity engender a state of awe. This is what people are after when they attend a festival, a rave, a concert, or even a museum or natural wonder. It's not just a fleeting high but the dissolution of self, and a sense of connection to everything else.

As scientists are currently learning, an experience of awe makes a person more generous while also regulating cytokines for a more balanced immune response. Cultivated awe means creating opportunities for people to shift from the short-lived pleasure of an online hit (dopamine) to the longer-term social openness of true connection (oxytocin).

Awe means experiencing oneself as part of something greater. In the current, individualist mindset, such connection is frightening: it seems like a diminishment of one's individuality and freedom. Awe, intimacy, and group consciousness appear to compromise self-sovereignty and claims to ownership. In actuality, awe opens us to the fuller realization that our individual and collective identities are mutually reinforcing. Instead of embracing awe, however, the frightened individual panics. We build walls instead of tearing them down.

I discussed the difference between panic and awe at length in my book *Present Shock*. I described the way digital technology "collapses" narrative, and suggested how this could lead vulnerable people toward paranoid and conspiratorial substitutes for linear story. Here in America, we have seen that sad possibility play out even worse than I feared.

Instead of doubling down on the extractive and distracting technologies that substitute shots of adrenaline for awe, we must employ styles of education and arts that engender more of an embrace of the moment. We can build tolerance for a sustainable present by seeking out and maintaining experiences of awe. This means creating theater, film, TV, research, and education that promote the collective dynamic over individual assessment and achievement. We must encourage the creation of art and culture that is recalibrating, and technology that is nonabrasive to the nervous system.

Like any human experience, the state of awe is inaccessible to machines. Artificial intelligences cannot care about people, however we program them, because they have no experience of anything at all. At the very least, embracing awe and doing so in front of our machines will demonstrate to them that there's a dimension of our experience that we value and that they must learn to prioritize—even if it is invisible to them.

We must stop using technology on people in an effort to program them, and instead provide the tools, sensibilities, socialization, and courage we need to program the world ourselves, together.

A special note to educators: The Intelligent Use of Artificial Intelligence

I finally received one. It was clear as day.

A student in my Propaganda course at Queens College who had barely been able to construct a sentence all semester turned in a final paper with perfect organization and zero punctuation errors. It was as if someone else had written the paper.

That someone was AI.

In previous semesters, I had occasionally encountered papers downloaded from web-based services or simply cut-and-paste from essays, articles, or even Wikipedia. They were easy enough to find with a simple web search. As if wanting to be caught, some students have even turned in papers written by other students for previous semesters of my course.

Because I teach at a public college, most of my students are not wealthy enough to hire tutors or the online academic version of taskrabbits to write their papers for them. (A friend of mine who teaches at an elite high school once challenged a student to answer a few basic questions about such a paper, to see if he even understood what was on the page.

The student's parents complained, and the teacher was put on suspension for traumatizing the boy.)

AI chat platforms level the playing field, giving students without the money to pay for bespoke papers from anonymous graduate-student gig workers an opportunity to produce and submit essays they haven't written. So far, the results are not at what we would normally consider college level. Yes, the sentences are clear, and the organization of the papers is good. Many of my college students have not had the opportunity to learn the basics of nouns, verbs, sentences, and paragraphs, so these papers do stand out. Compared with many of the papers I receive, which have been produced through speech-to-text with no proofreading, the AI-produced essays are of professional caliber.

So far, at least to an experienced essay reader, they all exhibit telltale signs of synthetic production. The depth of analysis remains exactly constant. There are no "aha" moments, no incomplete thoughts, no wrestling with ambiguity. It all reads like a Wikipedia article (no doubt where much of the "thinking" has been derived, at least indirectly).

Still, without proof, it's hard to accuse a student of writing a paper that looks and feels like it has been generated by AI. And the AI's will no doubt get better with time. So what's a teacher to do? Assuming we care, that grades matter, and that as accrediting institutions we need to enforce basic academic integrity, there are a few good alternatives.

First, and easiest, are free online analytical tools where you can paste the text and determine how predictable each word of the essay is based on the ones it followed. The more predictable the words, the more likely they were produced by an AI. One platform highlights predictable words in green, and more surprising terms (human ones—what most tech people would call "noise," but what I would call "signal") in yellow or red.

But I think the problem of students submitting fraudulently produced papers points to a more fundamental issue with how we do education. Instead of entering a technological arms race against cheating students, we need to shift our approach to achievement and assessment. Many professors I know who were educated in Europe had never encountered a Scantron answer sheet before coming to the United States. For them, the essay submitted by a student is not the culmination of a semester's work, but the starting place for a conversation.

Our model of education, with students taking tests and writing essays to "prove" their competency in order to get a passing grade and "credit" toward a degree, is itself a one-size-fits-all artifact of the Industrial Age. I understand why we might want to give competency exams to paramedics and cab drivers before entrusting them with our lives, but a liberal arts education is not a license to practice; it is an invitation to engage with ideas, culture, and society.

That's a hard culture to engender with fifty or more students in a "seminar," or several hundred in a lecture, particularly when many colleges can no longer afford teaching assistants or graduate students to help read papers. It's even harder when students are showing up more for the credit than the learning. But the only truly workable response to a student population that has turned to AI to produce its papers is to retrieve the time-consuming, face-to-face interaction that (for me, anyway) constituted the most memorable moments of my education.

Yes, I'm talking about live conversations with students about their ideas, their perspectives on what they have read, or even their responses to my questions about their work. In some sense, we can see the way students have resorted to AI-produced essays as an entirely utilitarian response to an educational culture that has become far too utilitarian, itself. If we want our students to bring their human selves to the table, we must create an educational environment that fosters human engagement.

AI will force us to make education more human.

This doesn't mean avoiding AI in the classroom, but rather embracing it as yet another tool that will become increasingly available to our students in their research, work, and lives. We need to show them that offloading the drudgery of a task to technology actually frees up more capacity for them to do the truly human part of any task. Rather than simply turning them into cheaters by replacing their work, AI can upskill our students—but only if we as educators are ready to upskill our teaching methods as well.

First, if we want our students to see their education as something more than a line on their LinkedIn profile, we must transcend the utilitarian nature of our assignments. We have to tell our students why they are being given an assignment, and judge them not solely on the quality of their output but the extent to which they achieved their learning goal. How has writing that paper changed and improved their ability to think, talk, and argue about the topic?

Second, and probably more important, we should give students the option of using AI as a resource and writing partner. You want to use AI for your paper? Fine. Then your assignment is to get the AI to write a paper with which you entirely agree.

Using AI means learning how to iterate until you get the result you want—a result you are willing to stand by and defend.

This is as true for STEM classes as liberal arts. Students in programming classes should be able to use AI for their code assignments, with the caveat that they ask the AI to provide several different coding strategies. The student must then choose the one they think is best, and explain how and why they made that choice. Just like businesses, students can either outsource their competencies to AI and become obsolete, or partner with AI to develop skills on the next level.

Teachers must learn to feel comfortable with students employing AI throughout their studies in the same way they might employ a calculator, Wikipedia, or a spellchecker. I'm less concerned with students cheating with AI than with how our own refusal to engage with AI in the classroom will be cheating our students of the sensibilities they will need to succeed in the future.

ESSENTIAL READING

BOOKS

Doctorow, Cory and Rebecca Giblin. *Chokepoint Capitalism: How Big Tech and Big Content Captured Creative Labor Markets and How We'll Win Them Back*. Boston: Beacon Press, 2023.

Heitner, Devorah. *Growing Up in Public: Coming of Age in a Digital World*. New York: TarcherPerigee, 2023.

Innis, Harold. *The Bias of Communication*. Toronto, Ontario: University of Toronto Press, 2008. [First published in 1951.]

Kelly, Kevin. *What Technology Wants*. New York: Viking, 2010.

Lanier, Jaron. *You Are Not a Gadget*. New York: Knopf, 2009.

Lawrence Lessig. *Free Culture: The Nature and Future of Creativity*. New York: Penguin, 2005.

McLuhan, Marshall. *Understanding Media*. New York: McGraw-Hill, 1964.

Noble, Safiya Umaja. *Algorithms of Oppression: How Search Engines Reinforce Racism*. New York: NYU Press, 2018.

Packer, Randall and Ken Jordan. *Multimedia: From Wagner to Virtual Reality*. New York: Norton, 2001. See the essays by Vannevar Bush, Norbert Weiner, James Licklider, Douglas Englebart, Ted Nelson, Alan Kay, and other Internet pioneers and visionaries.

Postman, Neil. *Technopoly: The Surrender of Culture to Technology*. New York: Vintage Books, 1993.

Rheingold, Howard. *The Virtual Community: Homesteading on the Electronic Frontier*. Cambridge: MIT Press, 1993.

Rushkoff, Douglas. *Cyberia: Life in the Trenches of Hyperspace*. San Francisco: HarperCollins, 1994.

Rushkoff, Douglas. *Survival of the Richest: Escape Fantasies of the Tech Billionaires*. New York: W. W. Norton, 2022.

Rushkoff, Douglas. *Throwing Rocks at the Google Bus: How Growth Became the Enemy of Prosperity*. New York: Portfolio, 2016.

Shiffman, Daniel. *Learning Processing: A Beginner's Guide to Programming Images, Animation, and Interaction*. San Francisco: Morgan Kaufmann, 2008.

Shirky, Clay. *Here Comes Everybody*. New York: Penguin, 2009.

Shlain, Tiffany. *24/6: The Power of Unplugging One Day a Week*. New York: Gallery Books, 2019.

Stephenson, Neal. *In the Beginning Was the Command Line*. New York: HarperCollins, 1999.

Turkle, Sherry. *Alone Together: Why We Expect More from Technology and Less from Each Other*. New York: Basic Books, 2011.

Wark, McKenzie. *A Hacker Manifesto*. Cambridge: Harvard University Press, 2004.

Weiner, Norbert. *The Human Use of Human Beings: Cybernetics and Society.* Cambridge: Da Capo Press, 1988. [First published in 1950.]

Zittrain, Jonathan. *The Future of the Internet--And How to Stop It.* New Haven: Yale University Press, 2009.

Zuboff, Shoshana. *The Age of Surveillance Capitalism: The Fight for a Human Future at the New Frontier of Power.* New York: PublicAffairs, 2019.

DOCUMENTARIES

Karim Amer and Jehane Noujaim, dir. *The Great Hack.* 2019, Netflix.

David Briggs, dir. *The Secret Rules of Modern Living: Algorithms.* 2015, BBC Four. https://www.bbc.co.uk/programmes/p030s6b3.

Cullen Hoback, dir. *Terms and Conditions May Apply.* 2013, Los Angeles, CA, Hyrax Films.

Jeff Orlvosky, dir. *The Social Dilemma.* 2020, Netflix.

Frontline. Season 2014, Episode 4, "Generation Like." Aired February 18, 2014, PBS. https://www.pbs.org/video/frontline-generation/.

Frontline. Season 2010, Episode 9, "Digital Nation." Produced by Rachel Dretzen and Douglas Rushkoff. Aired February 2, 2012, PBS. https://www.pbs.org/wgbh/frontline/documentary/digitalnation/.

The Virtual Revolution [series]. Aired January 30–February 20, 2010, BBC Two. https://www.bbc.co.uk/programmes/b00n4j0r/episodes/guide.

FREE RESOURCES TO LEARN PROGRAMMING

Code.org—http://code.org.

Codecademy—https://www.codecademy.com/.

Free Code Camp—http://freecodecamp.com.

Scratch—MIT's site for kids, but easy enough for adults: http://scratch.mit.edu/.

Skillcrush Coding Camp—https://learn.skillcrush.com/ skillcrush-free-bootcamp/.

Learn Python the Hard Way—A very accessible approach to a very useful computer language: http:// learnpythonthehardway.com/index.

Learning Processing—Tutorials by Daniel Shiffman: http:// www.learningprocessing.com.

SIMPLE—Some Apple II developers wrote this beginners' language back in 1995: http://www.simplecodeworks. com.

Microsoft Tutorials on Visual Basic—Microsoft's tutorials on how to learn Visual Basic are actually quite good for the beginner: http://msdn.microsoft.com/en-us/vbasic/ ms789097.aspx.

LOGOS—For educators interested in a very easy programming language to teach elementary school children, visit http://www.terrapinlogo.com for a system to purchase or http://www.softronix.com/logo.html for free resources.

For more up-to-date information, see http://rushkoff.com/ program.

Named one of the "world's ten most influential intellectuals" by MIT, Douglas Rushkoff is an author and documentarian who studies human autonomy in a digital age. His twenty other books include *Survival of the Richest*, *Team Human*, based on his podcast, *Present Shock*, and *Throwing Rocks at the Google Bus*. He also made the PBS *Frontline* documentaries *Generation Like*, *The Persuaders*, and *Merchants of Cool*. He won the Marshall McLuhan Award, as well as the Neil Postman Award for Career Achievement in Public Intellectual Activity. He is director of the MA program in Media Studies at the City University of New York, Queens College.

Printed in the USA
CPSIA information can be obtained
at www.ICGtesting.com
JSHW021240071124
PP13800600001B/2